# Scarred for LIFE!

# Scarred for LIFE!

XULON PRESS

# Scarred for Life!

## Written by:
## Tim Fletcher

### Psalms 103:1-5 (NIV)

Praise the lord, my Soul,
all my inmost being, praise his holy name.
Praise the Lord, my soul,
and forget not all his benefits
who forgives all your sins
and heals all your diseases,
who redeems your life from the pit
and crowns you with love and compassion,
who satisfies your desires with good things
so that your youth is renewed like the eagle's.

Xulon Press
2301 Lucien Way #415
Maitland, FL 32751
407.339.4217
www.xulonpress.com

© 2019 by Tim Fletcher

All rights reserved solely by the author. The author guarantees all contents are original and do not infringe upon the legal rights of any other person or work. No part of this book may be reproduced in any form without the permission of the author. The views expressed in this book are not necessarily those of the publisher.

Author's Disclaimer: This is my story and (unless you remember differently) I am sticking with it! Some stories have been condensed for the application. Names have been automatically removed because it is not meant to be accusatory in any way.

Unless otherwise indicated, Scripture quotations taken from the Holy Bible, New International Version (NIV). Copyright © 1973, 1978, 1984, 2011 by Biblica, Inc.™. Used by permission. All rights reserved.

Scripture taken from The Passion Translation (TPT). Copyright © 2017 by Passion & Fire Ministries, Inc. Used by permission. All rights reserved. thePassionTranslation.com

First Publishing, 2019
Printed in the United States of America.

ISBN-13: 978-1-54566-901-3

# Contents

| | |
|---|---|
| 09 | Prologue |
| 16 | The Experience |
| 20 | The Accident Scene |
| 24 | Back at Home |
| 27 | The Emergency Room |
| 36 | The Aftermath |
| 44 | The Routine |
| 49 | 4th of July |
| 53 | The War on Infection |
| 56 | Skin Grafting Begins |
| 72 | My First Trip Out of the Burn Unit |
| 90 | Home to Recover |
| 99 | Reality Sets In |
| 120 | The Consequences |
| 126 | The Origin of Scars |
| 131 | The Importance of Scars In Our |
| 137 | Lives Scars In the Bible |

# Dedication

I dedicate this book to the Glory of God, The Faithfulness of Jesus Christ and the Power of The Holy Spirit! May His Name be Glorified through the telling of what really is His story!

I also dedicate it to my Awesome life partner and wife, Debbie Fletcher. I am completely convinced God made her for me!! There isn't another woman who could have loved and supported me as she has through the last 44 years. This book is a testament to what can happen when a woman dedicates her life to praying for and loving a man as Debbie does me. Thank you, Babe!

# Foreword

What can I tell you about this book and the man who wrote it? Tim Fletcher is a man with great knowledge and personal insight into what it really means to be Scarred for Life... Tim has faced many adversities and great challenges while still a young boy, teenager and then a grown man. The story that he shares with you is true and everyone will find some truth applicable for themselves within its pages. It has been my sincere and great privilege to watch him grow into the man that he is today... a man that continually works to turn the many adversities within his life to victories... Tim is a man of great faith in God and his Lord and Savior Jesus Christ, as well as is a loving husband, father, and grandfather.

Tim has worn many different hats so to speak through the years... from the blueprint making boy I fell in love with, to a heavy equipment operator and truck driver, campground builder and manager, ambulance driver, Advanced First Aid and CPR instructor, as well as Pastor and loyal friend to all... (Human as well and pet). It has been my privilege to love, live with and work alongside this man for over 44 years. We've played together as young children, cried, laughed and learned to pray together as adults. I am truly Blessed to call this man my best friend and love of my life.

I encourage you to read the life-changing message that this book brings to light and challenge you to not find something within its pages to relate to and then find hope in for yourself. I've watched him lament and pour over its message of life-giving hope and know that this simple story can/will bring healing to your own wounds and see the scars that you carry in your own life in a new and even possibly purposeful way.

May God Bless You All,

With Loving Tribute,

Debbie Fletcher

# Acknowledgments

While it is absolutely impossible to acknowledge everyone in a story as large as this, I would like to try to bring recognition to as many as possible. As is always the danger when you mention one person's name there is always someone you will fail to mention. In advance, please forgive me if I have inadvertently overlooked anyone who should be recognized. Be assured God will reward each of you accordingly for your part in this story.

First, thank you to all the Prayer Warriors around the world who spent hours in prayer for my recovery. A short list of names starting with my mother, Bonnie Fletcher and then my wife, Debbie (Lingle) Fletcher, and her mother Margaret Lingle-Mossman. The Mighty Prayer Warriors of First Assembly of God church in Niles, Michigan who prayed for protection and healing not only for me but for my family and the nurses and doctors involved in my care as well. To those outside of the church I attended who joined them in prayer, you are not forgotten... Thank you.

Second but just as important, thank you to all my family and friends as well as neighbors who toiled endlessly taking care of my brother, Andrew, and sister, Pam while dad worked and he and mom cared for me in Ann Arbor. You allowed my mom to stay with me without interruption for over 3 months. I can't begin to express my gratitude for your thoughtfulness.

Next, to the men and women, doctors and nurses, staff and support team members who worked tirelessly and endlessly around the clock in what is now known as The Trauma/Burn Center of the University Of Michigan Hospital. I thank God every day for your consistent care and concern that you extended to me and my family while we were in your care.

Thank you to my many friends in and around the community as well as the youth group of First Assembly Of God Church who helped raise funds and supported me through cards, letters, prayer and keeping Debbie encouraged through it all.

Thank you to my father, Bruce Fletcher, who continued to work to support our family. For walking me around and around that fireplace in our house and kept me moving when that was the last thing I wanted to do. To the many visitors who came to the house and spent hours with me, especially my cousins, Jeff and Teresa who played Monopoly and Parcheesi with me endlessly. A special mention to school teachers, William Mitchell and Louis Milley who made a special trip to share a smile and encourage me when I first arrived back home.

A huge thank you to my wife Debbie who relived the painful memories of a not so pleasant time in our lives as well as to my college professor, Kathryn DeVore who along with Debbie have patiently endured my lack of writing skills. Also, my grand-daughter McKenzie Fletcher for her invaluable help in the 11th hour to finish the small details of the publishing process and for the design of the awesome cover.

To my brother, Andrew, Rev. Bob Renner, Rev. Duane Roth, Rev. Rodger Peck, and Rev. Terry Powell thank you for taking the time to read the manuscript and to respond with such kind words. Your friendships are invaluable to me.

And last but most importantly, Thank you, Jesus Christ, for healing me and then helping me to recognize the very special blessing you bestowed on me with the scars that have brought me LIFE and a LIFE LIVED MORE ABUNDANTLY!!!

# Introduction

You noticed the title, didn't you? The word "Scarred" caught your eye and you wanted to see the story behind the scars. This is the conundrum we find ourselves in every time we see someone with physical scars. We are intrigued to hear their story but want to turn away, so they don't see us looking at the scars their story left behind. If we look too closely, they may see we too are scarred. We work so hard to hide our scars the last thing we want to happen is for someone to see our own scars.

I am one of those people who when you look at me you notice my physical scars. You tend to look away or to pretend you didn't notice the scars I have on my body. When I draw attention to my scarred hands, people regularly respond with, "Oh, I didn't even notice them!"

Thousands of people have said this to me since the injury happened that left my body almost totally "Scarred!" People almost always ask what caused the scars that they can see. Only one or two have ever asked about the emotional or mental scars I carry within, and no one has ever asked what the scars themselves have caused!

I would like to share with you...both stories.

# Introduction

You noticed the title, didn't you? The word "Scarred" caught your eye and you wanted to see the story behind the scars. This is the conundrum we find ourselves in every time we see someone with physical scars. We are intrigued to hear their story but want to turn away, so they don't see us looking at the scars their story left behind. If we look too closely, they may see we too are scarred. We work so hard to hide our scars the last thing we want to happen is for someone to see our own scars.

I am one of those people who when you look at me you notice my physical scars. You tend to look away or to pretend you didn't notice the scars I have on my body. When I draw attention to my scarred hands, people regularly respond with, "Oh, I didn't even notice them!"

Thousands of people have said this to me since the injury happened that left my body almost totally "Scarred!" People almost always ask what caused the scars that they can see. Only one or two have ever asked about the emotional or mental scars I carry within, and no one has ever asked what the scars themselves have caused!

I would like to share with you...both stories.

# Prologue

I have been scarred for most of my life. For the most part, my scars haven't bothered me. When I was five or six, I put my hand through a storm door which left a major scar on my right arm. At eight or nine I was bitten by a dog. The dog took off half my nose and a part of my cheek. After that healed I had cosmetic surgery done. The doctors did a good job, although, even with the surgery, you can look at me and tell that my nose is uneven. I only remember a couple times in my life where somebody brought attention to the scars on my face.

The impact of having scars all over became extremely more focused because of the events that took place on May 26, 1972. Because of that accident, my body is almost completely covered in scars. I want to share with you the story of those scars. I also want to share what my experiences have been by being so scarred and when I've let Him, how God used this scarred body for His glory.

I was sixteen at the time of the accident. I was in love and loving life. At the time I had two goals for my life: Debbie Lingle and to drive something. Debbie and I had only dated a couple of times, but I knew I was head over heels in love with her. I know now, I didn't have a clue what that really meant. I had managed to get her class ring away from her, so I could say we were "going steady." She told me later we did not trade class rings but that I took hers and then made her take mine. Oh well, whatever works, right? It had taken me quite a while to get the nerve up to ask her out, so I guess I felt under pressure to get her commitment before she slipped away.

Debbie and I had just about grown up together. Her family came to our church when she was three and I was four years old. Both of our families were very active in the church we attended, so we saw a lot of each other up until she was thirteen and her father passed away. Her family left the church following her dad's funeral. They attended elsewhere for about a year until Easter morning 1971 when she showed up for Sunday morning service.

When I walked out of my Sunday School classroom at the front of our church, I was positive I was experiencing an angelic visitation. There in the back of the sanctuary sat the most beautiful angel I had ever seen. (Not that I had seen any angels before her!) I walked to the back of the church and introduced myself and totally ignoring the other guys sitting with her, asked if she would like to come into our Sunday School class. Not realizing that one of the gentlemen she was sitting with already had plans for her life, my invitation was refused. The next week she didn't bring her boyfriend, and she did come into class. I was happy although it took me almost a year to get the backbone enough to ask her out. We spent a lot of time together at church youth group activities and meetings, and we eventually dated several times before that Sunday afternoon when we "traded" class rings.

The same week we "traded Class rings" a week of evangelistic services started at our church. On that following Wednesday, I was able to make the trip to Galien (about a 30-mile round trip) to pick up Debbie and bring her back to Niles for church and then take her back home. We experienced a wonderful week with God working in both of our lives.

On Wednesday evening following the sermon, I was at the altar. I was asking God for two things: one, the infilling of the Holy Spirit with the evidence of speaking in tongues or any other evidence God had for me. Second, that God would give me a testimony as great as my dad's. It was at this same time in my life while listening to a missionary talking about taking Bibles into China that I felt my first nudge toward a life of full-time ministry. I felt God just might be calling me to drive a truck hauling Bibles.

On Thursday, again after listening to the sermon the evangelist had shared, I was back at the altar seeking the same two things from God. With several people supporting me in prayer God filled me with His Holy Spirit. The second thing I had been asking God for would begin the very next day.

The next day, Friday, May 26, 1972, started out more or less normal for me. Because my parents had gone up north to hunt mushrooms, I was staying at my friends Ted and Tim's house. My sister Pam and my brother Andrew had been staying at our neighbor's home across the street from ours. After school, I came home excited about buying a 1967 Chevy Impala I had put some money down on just before my parents left. Up until that time I had been either riding my motorcycle or driving one of my parents' cars.

My brother and sister had joined me back at our house after school. I was supposed to be mowing while Pam was watching our little brother and we waited for my parents to get home. I was excited about going to town and getting the car. Being anxious that my parents wouldn't return in time to go to the bank before it closed, I finally decided to send my sister and brother to the neighbors across the street. My plan was to go to the bank and pick up my money and be ready to pick up the car before I met Debbie at church.

My father was an excavating contractor and had a gas pump at our house. I started my trip by filling up my motorcycle with gas before heading in to town. On the way, I decided to stop by my friend Mike's and ask him if he wanted to ride with me to the bank and I would drop him off on evidence God had for me. Second, that God would give me a testimony as great as my dad's. It was at this same time in my life while listening to a missionary talking about taking Bibles into China that I felt my first nudge toward a life of full-time ministry. I felt God just might be calling me to drive a truck hauling Bibles.

On Thursday, again after listening to the sermon the evangelist had shared, I was back at the altar seeking the same two things from God. With several people supporting me in prayer God filled me with His Holy Spirit. The second thing I had been asking God for would begin the very next day.

The next day, Friday, May 26, 1972, started out more or less normal for me. Because my parents had gone up north to hunt mushrooms, I was staying at my friends Ted and Tim's house. My sister Pam and my brother Andrew had been staying at our neighbor's home across the street from ours. After school, I came home excited about buying a 1967 Chevy Impala I had put some money down on just before my parents left. Up until that time I had been either riding my motorcycle or driving one of my parents' cars.

My brother and sister had joined me back at our house after school. I was supposed to be mowing while Pam was watching our little brother and we waited for my parents to get home. I was excited about going to town and getting the car. Being anxious that my parents wouldn't return in time to go to the bank before it closed, I finally decided to send my sister and brother to the neighbors across the street. My plan was to go to the bank and pick up my money and be ready to pick up the car before I met Debbie at church.

My father was an excavating contractor and had a gas pump at our house. I started my trip by filling up my motorcycle with gas before heading in to town. On the way, I decided to stop by my friend Mike's and ask him if he wanted to ride with me to the bank and I would drop him off on the way back home. He declined, and I went on. Leaving his house put me ten blocks from the bank and six blocks from my new future.

# The Experience

## Change For A Lifetime

**D**owntown was fairly crowded with traffic and people. It was 4:00 PM on the Friday of Memorial Day weekend. I was going south on Front street when I passed a northbound motorcycle just like mine. This was surprising because there weren't a lot of bikes around like my Suzuki 90. It was orange and on a full-size frame giving it the look of a larger bike. It also had an eight-speed transmission with four high-range gears and four low range gears for off-road trail riding. In 1972, the way to wave was a raised fist in the air so I raised my fist and nodded my head to them. There were two people on the bike. As we went by each other I turned and watched them. I studied their bike for way too long. Then it happened, before I looked forward I hit the back of a car which had stopped for traffic in front of me.

I remember thinking, "Oh my goodness, I've had an accident!" I can't say I was panicked, but I was concerned. I felt my head and helmet slide across the trunk and hit the back window of the car before I fell off the right side of the car to the pavement. I wasn't going very fast, probably twenty-five miles per hour at the most. Immediately after hitting the ground I began to pick myself up and basically just shake off the impact. I didn't think (and I still don't believe) I was hurt very badly. I was way more concerned about my bike that was lying in the road. Although my bike was totaled, I don't remember having any pain at the moment of impact.

I got up on my knees, and I think I had one hand on the car door and looked through the window of the car. There was a lady in the car with a couple of children. I must have been in shock because I also hadn't realized I was soaked in gasoline from the motorcycle which had lost its gas cap. Without any warning, I heard the "Swoosh" of igniting gasoline and the whole world was on fire.

I remember saying to myself, "Oh God! I'm on fire!" This had to be a prayer because I never took the Lord's name in vain. My mind raced with thoughts of how to put the fire (me) out. All I could see was flames in front of my eyes. I had this feeling of melting and I could feel my skin coming off my body. All I could think of was, I can't lay down and roll here because I'm on pavement. I must get to the side road up ahead which was dirt.

Suddenly, I heard a voice say, "Lay down and roll!" I responded, "Which way?" The voice said, "I don't care, just roll!" and I did. I immediately started feeling people hit me with coats. They continued to tell me to roll, and they continued to beat me with what I found out later was a leather jacket, a suit coat, and a shirt. Months later after I got out of the hospital I spoke to Roger and Jim, two of the many people who helped me that day. They both told of how they had to beat out the flames and how horrible it was. They said one guy had taken his shirt off and hit me once, and when he went to hit the flames again his shirt was gone from the heat. Finally, the fire was out for a second, and then it re-ignited, and it did again the third time before it was out for good.

# The Accident Scene

As soon as the fire was out, one of the two men told me they had to get my clothes off me because they were still smoldering. Also, what kept re-igniting the fire was a small flame that was inside my biker's boots. I responded, "Ok, take the clothes but whatever you do don't cut the belt." "Just take the buckle loose and take it off." The next thing I hear is a hissing noise, and I think some cursing. When Roger stopped by the house seven or eight started feeling people hit me with coats. They continued to tell me to roll, and they continued to beat me with what I found out later was a leather jacket, a suit coat, and a shirt. Months later after I got out of the hospital I spoke to Roger and Jim, two of the many people who helped me that day. They both told of how they had to beat out the flames and how horrible it was. They said one guy had taken his shirt off and hit me once, and when he went to hit the flames again his shirt was gone from the heat. Finally, the fire was out for a second, and then it re-ignited, and it did again the third time before it was out for good.

# The Accident Scene

As soon as the fire was out, one of the two men told me they had to get my clothes off me because they were still smoldering. Also, what kept re-igniting the fire was a small flame that was inside my biker's boots. I responded, "Ok, take the clothes but whatever you do don't cut the belt." "Just take the buckle loose and take it off." The next thing I hear is a hissing noise, and I think some cursing. When Roger stopped by the house seven or eight months later he showed me the scar on his palm where he attempted to pull off the belt. The buckle was so hot it branded his palm. He told me he had to cut the belt because it was too hot to take off. He said when he took off what was left of my jeans, my skin came with them. He knew then he had to cut my boots off also because he was afraid he would pull the skin off my whole foot while trying to remove them. He finally got what remained of my clothes off me.

An off-duty nurse who had been shopping in the store where this had just taken place in front of, ran back in and got a couple sheets, soaked them in water and put them over me. This both protected me from exposure and from foreign objects. It also began cooling my skin. Roger said the only real complaint I had was that "my elbows hurt." I remember him squatting over me and letting me put my elbows on his shoes. He said that he could feel the heat coming off me through his shoes.

I don't remember a lot of shouting or panicking at the time. Roger kept talking to me keeping me calm. Finally, an officer showed up. I remember him asking for my driver's license. Roger exploded! And his language was getting very vulgar. Roger cussed at him and told him to go get the ambulance. Surprisingly the officer left and checked on the other emergency vehicles. When he came back, he said they needed to get my helmet off. Roger started swearing again and told the officer absolutely not and asked what was taking the fire department and ambulance so long? He again told the officer to go help the emergency vehicles get through traffic faster. The officer didn't leave but did back off and no longer interfered with the care I was receiving.

When the fire truck showed up the firemen started talking about taking off my helmet. I complained that nobody was getting my bike out of the road. They tried to assure me it was protected, but I wasn't convinced. I remember one of the firemen saying, "we need to crack that helmet to take it off." I immediately started arguing that they couldn't crack it because I couldn't replace it and it was very special to me. Some years later after sharing this part of the story a retired fireman walked up to me and said that accident was his first accident scene. I said, "Wow, were you ever on the scene of any worse?" He said, "Not where the victim survived."

It wasn't long, and the ambulance arrived. They loaded me up, and we made the five-block trip to the hospital. In 1972, ambulance transportation had not changed much from the 1950s when they were transporting my dad from the "wrecks" he had been in. They put you in the back and away they went. No triage, no IV's, nothing but drive as fast as you could, and they did! Because of the traffic of the holiday weekend, they cut through two parking lots rocking the unit a lot. I felt every bit of it. It was a rough ride. I drove for another ambulance service years later and every time I had a patient on board and I was driving, I thought of that ride.

# Back at Home

This part of the story is taken from the many times I heard dad and mom tell it. Mom and Dad had been in Honor, Michigan, about 4 hours north of where we lived, hunting mushrooms. They said they had noticed how peaceful the trip was. Being in the woods communing with the Lord and nature and the time together had been a good experience.

At the same time, they both had been plagued with nightmares every night. They both told of dreaming about storms and storm clouds off in the distance and the feeling of impending doom.

This wasn't new to them. Mom and Dad had lost five children when the children were very young. The youngest child was stillborn and the oldest of the five was three and a half (3 ½), she died from complications related to polio. It seemed to them that whenever they were about to go through a difficult time in their life, God would prepare them with a warning in their sleep. They had experienced this phenomenon in their life enough to know it was meant to be a time of prayer and fasting for them.

They were planning on staying for most of the day and traveling home late expecting to get home after supper. As they hunted on this Friday, they found a few pounds of mushrooms and were sitting on a log out in the woods just being quiet. Mom said, "Well, I think it's time to go home." Dad said later that he had felt it, too. Just a nudge from God that whatever was coming was happening now. Dad agreed, and they started their journey home.

Mom and Dad arrived back at our home town about 4 PM and went straight to the neighbor's house across the street to pick up my brother and sister. While they were there, a Michigan State Police car pulled into our driveway. The trooper got out of the car and was looking around. Dad waved him over to where they were.

After identifying Mom and Dad, the trooper explained he didn't know any particulars but that I had been in an accident, and that he would escort them to the hospital. Dad knew from how fast he drove it wasn't going to be good.

# The Emergency Room

I had been in the emergency room for a while before Mom and Dad got there. The hospital had called our family doctor, Dr. Fred Lindenfeld, to come and he was there treating me and getting ready to move me to a place where they were better prepared to treat an injury like mine.

The nurses had been asking me for my parent's names and a home phone number. I had constantly refused to give them the number and begged them NOT to call home. I told them my parents were out of town and that only my younger sister was home with my little brother and I didn't want them to scare either of them telling them I had been in a wreck. I truly thought I would still make it home before Mom and Dad. I never thought that I might be in the hospital overnight.

After asking several times I finally told the nurse to call my pastor. While most people referred to him as Pastor or Reverend, I always referred to him as, Brother Boland. He told me later that as soon as he heard the hospital was calling and someone was asking for "Brother" Boland he knew it was me. The hospital explained to him a little of what had happened, and he came to be with me and to be there until Mom and Dad arrived.

At the hospital, there was a lot of standing around looking at me. They had tried to get an IV started in my foot. The first one they tried wouldn't run. There wasn't enough circulation in that leg to allow the IV flow. Their second attempt in the other leg flowed but they weren't sure how long it would last. I remember them lifting the sheets covering me and discussing where they could get a viable line. One of the first dangers for a burn patient is dehydration and shock, so the IV was critical to my survival.

Mom and Dad finally arrived at the hospital. Dr. Lindenfeld came in and told me they were there and they would be in shortly. The sight of them walking into that hospital room will never leave my mind. When they walked in, Dad had his arm around mom making sure if she passed out she wouldn't fall. Dad had a look of brutal determination on his face. He was normally the tough one, but he knew this situation was going to try that determination like never before. Mom's whole countenance was pure pain. She was crying before she got into the room, but now as she tried to hold back the tears, I could see that her very soul was in agony. I have never seen her face in such agony before or since. The shock of what they saw lying there before them must have been overwhelming.

As the shock for mom and Dad wore off a little, my doctor began to explain how bad it really was. He lifted the sheets. Dad had to look, but mom turned her face as if to look away and then turned her eyes back again to see as little as possible and yet still be able to understand. Mom was overwhelmed with what she saw.

This is how I remember the doctor explaining it: "Tim has been burned with third-degree burns over most of his body. His legs, his arms, hands, chest, stomach, and back all have third-degree burns. The front of his neck and his chin are also burned. This all adds up to eighty-six percent (87%) of his body that has third-degree burns." After I had been released from the hospital I heard the formula they used at the time to determine the chances of surviving the burns. They took the percentage of third-degree burns, added your age, and then subtracted that from

100 and the answer resulted in the percentage chance of survival. When you added mine up the total was 103. I had a -3% chance of living.

While Dad had the look of determination on his face and mom originally was devastated that didn't last long. Mom began to talk to me, asking how I felt and asked if she could do anything for me. Her agony and devastation soon turned to resolve. No one knew it yet, but mom would not see home again until August, 3 months later. She remained with me constantly only going to an apartment they rented located near the hospital to sleep and pray.

My doctor soon called an orderly into the room and told him to get a plane ready that he wanted to fly me to the University of Michigan burn unit in Ann Arbor, Michigan. He went out and made several phone calls but could not find a plane. When he came back in and told Dr. Lindenfeld, he said, "Go look again and more! We must have a plane!" He went back out and made more calls. No response, there was nothing available.

Then, miraculously the hospital got a call from a man named Art Perez who worked at Tyler Refrigeration Corporation here in Niles. He said he had heard that the hospital was looking for an airplane to transport a seriously injured patient to another hospital and that there would be a plane standing by at the local airport ready to take off when they were.

The orderly was so excited when he got to tell my doctor he had a plane. Dr. Lindenfeld responded "Great, now get me another one, the parents are going to fly up at the same time and need a separate plane." He called Mr. Perez back and Mr. Perez gave us another plane. Years later, I got to meet Mr. Perez and thank him. He was a wonderful man.

Just before it was time to move me, my extended family began to arrive, my uncles and aunts. I don't remember them all being there, but I do remember my Uncle Charlie and Aunt Louise coming in. They both had tears in their eyes.

100 and the answer resulted in the percentage chance of survival. When you added mine up the total was 103. I had a -3% chance of living.

While Dad had the look of determination on his face and mom originally was devastated that didn't last long. Mom began to talk to me, asking how I felt and asked if she could do anything for me. Her agony and devastation soon turned to resolve. No one knew it yet, but mom would not see home again until August, 3 months later. She remained with me constantly only going to an apartment they rented located near the hospital to sleep and pray.

My doctor soon called an orderly into the room and told him to get a plane ready that he wanted to fly me to the University of Michigan burn unit in Ann Arbor, Michigan. He went out and made several phone calls but could not find a plane. When he came back in and told Dr. Lindenfeld, he said, "Go look again and more! We must have a plane!" He went back out and made more calls. No response, there was nothing available.

Then, miraculously the hospital got a call from a man named Art Perez who worked at Tyler Refrigeration Corporation here in Niles. He said he had heard that the hospital was looking for an airplane to transport a seriously injured patient to another hospital and that there would be a plane standing by at the local airport ready to take off when they were.

The orderly was so excited when he got to tell my doctor he had a plane. Dr. Lindenfeld responded "Great, now get me another one, the parents are going to fly up at the same time and need a separate plane." He called Mr. Perez back and Mr. Perez gave us another plane. Years later, I got to meet Mr. Perez and thank him. He was a wonderful man.

Just before it was time to move me, my extended family began to arrive, my uncles and aunts. I don't remember them all being there, but I do remember my Uncle Charlie and Aunt Louise coming in. They both had tears in their eyes.

Either the shock or the medication was keeping me from realizing the gravity of what was going on. Uncle Charlie just said, "We'll see you when you get back." Aunt Louise couldn't talk. Uncle Jim came in. He had a way of standing kind of bent over and looking out the side of his eyes at you when he was disgusted. We always called it, "that Fletcher look!" He gave me one of those and I remember him as plain as day saying, "Son, you've sure done it now." Then in tears, he left, and it was time to move me back to the ambulance for the ride to the airport then to Ann Arbor.

Riding along with me in the ambulance were my parents and a nurse. The nurse had to go with me to Ann Arbor because of the IV and to take care of any other emergencies that would arise. I don't remember much about the ambulance ride to the airport, but I want to share the story my dad always tells about the ride: It's only a seven to eight-minute ride from the hospital to the airport in Niles when you have the assistance of emergency lights and sirens. About halfway there, Dad was praying not only that they would survive the ambulance ride but also that I would survive this whole ordeal. He said as they made a left-hand turn from Oak Street onto 13$^{th}$ Street he heard God say to him in an audible voice seven words, "He can live if you will believe!" He said the importance of believing even when circumstances said otherwise, was not always going to be easy. When we arrived at the airport there were two planes waiting there for us.

I remember the struggle they had getting me into the plane. They had removed the seats out of a single-engine plane and were trying to put me into it. I was six-foot-tall and the stretcher was just a little longer than I. The door opened the wrong way for the stretcher to go in easily or flat. I was sure I was going to get dumped off the stretcher onto the ground. But thanks to the perseverance and tenacity of the people putting me on the plane, I was finally loaded up and we were off to the Burn Center at the University of Michigan hospital. I don't remember anything about the flight or the ambulance ride from the Ann Arbor airport to the Burn Center, and when I spoke to the nurse who went with me, she said it was uneventful.

# The Aftermath

## The First Night In The Burn Unit

I vaguely remember getting to the burn unit that evening. I do remember coming to and realizing that somebody was hurting me. Up until this time, I don't remember any sensation of pain. The burns didn't hurt, they felt more like the sensation of melting. In the emergency room in Niles, the staff had tried to put IV's in my feet and that too hadn't hurt, but now somebody was hurting me and even with all the drugs I must have had in me, I knew they were doing something I didn't like.

First, they had to get an IV in me that could move the massive amount of fluid and medications I was going to need to keep me alive. In order to do this, they would use a "subclavian IV." This book is not intended to be a medical journal so please understand I am sharing what I remember and what I have learned from those who were around during the time that I went through this.

In order to place a subclavian IV, the doctors had to insert a subclavian catheter into my chest and guide it to the subclavian artery. This procedure began with three shots of Novocain into the site where the catheter went in. As time went on I learned to take the catheter without the Novocain because of how bad the Novocain hurt on my chest.

When they got the IV in they put me into a big whirlpool tub and began the process of cleaning the burned areas. This would be the next real battle I had to go through. After about a half hour in the tub they took me out and the second battle started, keeping me warm. Our skin is the largest organ of our body and it is the organ that is most effective to keep our temperature regulated. Mine was pretty much gone. As they got me out of the tub I began to shiver, and I think I shivered most of the next six months. I would soon be distracted by the first battle though.

When they got me out of the tub they put me on a gurney, covered me with a sheet and took me across a little hallway into an operating room where they proceeded to begin the manual debridement process. The debriding process was one of the worst but vitally crucial experiences of the whole time I was in the burn unit. A doctor would stand on either side of me and use a pair of tweezers and a scalpel to peel away the dead skin and all the debris that was left in and on the injury site. They had to perform this everywhere there were burns. This would be the most painful part of the healing process. At first, they were pulling old jean material and small stones and all sorts of stuff out of my body all the while cutting off the burned/dead skin.

One day I was lying on the operating table and there was a doctor on either side of me. I was complaining that one doctor was causing me pain. The doctor who was not hurting me began to pick on the one who was the source of my immediate discomfort. This really bothered the doctor who was causing the pain. Remember you don't work in the Burn Unit (or any major trauma unit) for the money. You work there because you care about people. Also, most of the doctors working in the Burn Unit were still in training. The doctor who was causing me so much discomfort began to watch the other one and try to adjust how he held the tools and how he cut away the debris in a real effort to stop hurting me as he worked. He wasn't able to do it as painlessly as the first doctor. So they changed sides. After getting new tweezers and scalpel they went back to work, but the first doctor still did his job almost painlessly and the second one still did something that caused pain as he worked. Actually, I really felt bad for him and gained a new appreciation for his heart attitude when treating patients.

While the doctors worked on the debridement process, they also had to make shallow cuts on my limbs and down both sides of my torso. This prepared my body for the swelling that would be caused by not only the injuries I had suffered but also by all the IV fluids they were putting in me.

They worked on the debridement process for about an hour. When they completed the debridement for the evening, they would take what they called a "Silver Solution" and dip a fine mesh gauze in it and wrap one smooth layer around all the areas that were burned. Then they would follow the fine gauze with a thicker gauze which they had also dipped in the Silver Solution and cover all the fine gauze. Then because my hands were severely burned, they had to put them in braces so they would hold their shape over the coming months of healing.

This was a very uncomfortable process. It seemed the braces were too big for my hands, and I didn't seem to have enough control over my arms and hands to get into the braces. Following the braces, they would cover everything with a dry covering of gauze and a bandage made like a cotton towel. This first night they put something in my eyes because of the heat and smoke and I was off to my bed.

My bed was a Circle Electric Bed. It was made of aluminum and allowed me to be turned from lying in a face-up position to either a standing position or to lying in a face-down position with very little effort. Once I got into the bed they had to tie my hands which were in braces to the bed frame to alleviate some of the swelling that was about to begin. I got into my bed about 9:00 that evening, almost five hours after my accident back in Niles. No one realized that it would be six months before I would get to leave and go back home.

When the doctors and nurses got me settled in my bed Mom and Dad were allowed in for a little while. It was an emotional time. Dad tells the following story.

The first person that mom and dad met was a tall nurse by the name of Rudy. Rudy was an extremely dedicated nurse, not only to the patient but also to the process of treating burn patients. Rudy must not have liked Mom and Dad being in the unit after visiting hours and must have said something to them more than once. From Mom and Dad's perspective, this was not the first time they had been in the hospital with a child in a "fight for your life" situation. To Dad, rules were made to be either broken or totally ignored depending on the severity of the injury. From Rudy's perspective, the rules were there to increase the possibility of survival in a place where survival wasn't all that common. Two strong-willed individuals who cared deeply for their patient were about to have a clash. At some point, Rudy reminded them again that visiting hours were over, and they needed to leave and come back in the morning. Dad stood his ground telling Rudy they would leave when they were ready and when they felt I was ready for them to leave and that everything centered on what was best for me.

Finally, Mom and Dad left the unit. Coming and going into the unit required some time. You had to be completely covered from head to toe with protective garments to limit the possibility of contaminating the patient with germs. As Mom and Dad made their way down the hall, Dad felt God nudge him to go back and apologize to Rudy. Dad walked back down to the unit and apologized. Rudy responded with a pat on the back and assured Dad everyone in the unit would do their absolute best to see their son to a complete recovery. Mom and Dad then made their way to the car which our pastor had driven up while I had been in the plane and being admitted to the Burn Unit, where they slept for a couple hours.

# The Routine

The burn unit was almost always full, and every patient was taken to the bathtub, bathed, and their dressings changed twice a day. While I was there, Thursday was also "operating day" when skin was removed for grafting purposes. While all of this was going on, they had new patients coming in at all hours. With all this activity there had to be a routine, or everything would erupt into mass chaos. On my first full day, I began to realize this wasn't going to be easy, and I wasn't sure I wanted to be here for the fight.

I woke up thirsty. Mom asked if I could have a drink of water. Mom and I were shown a 4-ounce cup of ice that I could chew or suck on for the next eight hours. Each shift the head nurse also brought in a shoebox full of medications that had to be put through the IV system hanging above my head. These included anti-biotics, anti-anxiety, vitamins, anti-itch, medications for swelling, anti-rejection medications for the grafts, and anticoagulation for blood clots and pain medications. All but one medication Heparin, went into the IV. Heperin went into my abdomen. Once Rudy told me that the nurses administered 38 different shots to me each shift. Along with all these meds, the team also poured the Silver Solution over me every couple of hours keeping my bandages moist.

My initial routine consisted of waking up in the morning, and mom coming in to feed me. The nurses immediately started getting me to feed myself with spoons and forks attached to tongue depressors taped to them so I could reach my mouth. Because of the thickness of the bandages, it was very difficult to bend my arms. It also hurt tremendously to bend them. Following breakfast, I would rest a couple minutes then they would come get me for my bath. That meant I got a pain shot which would not only alleviate some of the pain of removing the bandages but also help me take a nap. Bathe, dressings off, debridement, redress my wounds, and back to bed, followed by lunch. Not too long after I arrived they started trying to get me to walk. Walking was a nightmare in itself.

Every time the nurses would get me up to walk, (And they had to make me, or I wouldn't do it.) the blood vessels in my legs would pop open and I would bleed through the dressings on my legs. This would scare me beyond imagination. I would cry and carry on over these little bleeders like they had cut my leg off. I don't know how my mother stood it. Along with the bleeders, almost immediately I would get real dizzy which also scared me and made me want to get back into bed. The bleeding and the dizziness happened whether I was walking or sitting in a chair.

Another battle I had to wage was with my breathing. I would have breathing treatments a couple times a day. Again, I hated these treatments. I was only there a couple days when I started experiencing fluid build up in my lungs because I was not able to sit up long enough to get it out or absorb it through my body. These breathing treatments became more difficult as time passed. It didn't help that I almost refused to do them for mom on the weekends or any time the therapist wasn't available.

People tell me "I must have been a fighter!" I look back and think the fighter was Mom, Dad and those people who prayed day and night for me. I had unconsciously made a decision to float along, causing the least amount of personal strain or pain.

In the afternoon/evening I would get another bath which involved my dressings being removed, another round of debridement, rebandage and back to bed, eat supper and then try to sleep.

# The 4th Of July

The routine of day-to-day life in the burn unit went on and my recovery went well. The first major benchmark I needed to get to was to be healthy enough to start the skin grafting process. In the five weeks I had been there, I had begun making good progress toward that goal. The weekend of July 4th that all changed.

It must have been on that Saturday or Sunday that the Burn Unit began to run low on the Silver Solution that they applied to my gauze and poured over me every couple hours to keep my dressings wet. July 4th was on Tuesday that year so it was a real long weekend. The staff started using less and less of the solution to make it stretch. My progress started to decline. On Sunday a nurse that only worked every other weekend came in. She immediately gasped, "My God, what have they done to Tim?" I had declined to the point that she could see it in my face and demeanor.

It was about this point in the weekend that I called Dad to the side of my bed and told him I was going through the valley of the shadow of death.

He responded, "And we'll go through it with you!" Dad said later that the only encouraging thing he could hang onto was I stated I was "going through" not dying in this valley.

This book is not about accusations or calling out someone or some group for mistakes. I don't recall and never heard mom or dad place any type of blame on anyone for running short of the solution I needed. Here's what they would relate every time they told the story.

The Bible talks about entertaining angels unaware. Mom and dad believed some of those angels walked in and out of our lives every day in that burn unit in the form of the men and women who made up the doctors, nurses, and staff. Each one of them brought into our day-to-day life a unique and special personality or perspective that helped us as patients survive. On this weekend we saw them in action.

On Monday, some of the regular Monday-through-Friday nurses came in from the weekend even though it was technically still a holiday. Two of the male nurses were especially horrified at my condition and how much it had degraded. When they learned what was going on with the solution, they immediately started plotting a plan. Before we knew it, they had gotten into the warehouse where the medicine was located and brought enough to treat me and get me back on track to the health I was in before the holiday weekend started. At the beginning of the weekend, the doctors were talking about starting the skin grafting process the next week. By the end of the weekend, the grafting was put off for another month.

# The War On Infection

One of the biggest battles for a burn victim is the war on infection. The doctors are always strategizing, planning and scheming how to beat the biggest threat to the patient there is. For me, the most vulnerable place on my body was my left arm. It was by far the most severely burned. During the time I was in the Burn Unit I lost all five fingernails and the use of my thumb and most of the use of my pointer finger. This was where I was burned the very deepest.

Not long into our stay, the doctors came to Dad and discussed the idea of amputating my arm just below the elbow to ward off infection. Dad would ask if there was an infection there and they would respond, "Not at this time but it's primed for it."

Dad would come back with, "Let's wait one more week."

The next week the doctors would come to him again. We feel it is best for Tim's overall health to amputate his left arm an inch or two below his elbow to ward off infection. Dad again would ask if there was an infection there now and the doctors would say no.

He would simply repeat, "Let's wait another week."

Again, the following week the doctors came but this time they wanted to do the amputation just below the wrist.

Again, the question, "Is there any infection yet?"

"No." replied the doctors.

"Then" replied Dad, "Let's wait one more week."

The next week the same question and the same answer wanting to take the thumb and pointer finger. The same response waiting one more week.

I survived without the expected infection or having to have my arm amputated but infection was not the only battle I was to face.

# Skin Grafting Begins

Although the 4$^{th}$ of July weekend set me back, they continued the debridement process leaving a lot of uncovered and open wounds.

Another side-effect of the trauma of the 4$^{th}$ of July weekend was how much weight I had lost. By the end of July, I was down under 120 pounds even though I was slightly over 6 feet tall. The food at the hospital was not to my liking and usually was moderately cold by the time I got it. I pretty well lived on either Hot Dogs or

Hamburgers. Usually one for lunch and the other for supper. They came with fries but they were always cold by the time they made it to my room. To help me gain weight, Dad started bringing me chocolate malts quite regularly. This is definitely one of the better memories I have of the time I spent in the Burn Unit. Another not so pleasant memory is another habit Dad developed that didn't end very well…bringing me Watermelon!

Since I struggled with terrible thirst due to the fact of not being able to drink very much because of the large amounts of fluid going through the IV. Dad asked if I could have watermelon or was that also considered fluid? They didn't think it would cause any harm so Dad began to bring in watermelon. I love watermelon so of course, I ate it constantly. The staff even kept it in the refrigerator for me. I had it for several days in a row when all of a sudden the pressure around my heart skyrocketed.

The nurses would measure the pressure around my heart with an instrument that looked like a cross between a thermometer and a drinking straw. It fit into a three-way valve in my IV. It was about sixteen inches tall and measured in increments to about forty. Normal was around zero. There was not any danger up to about 10. On one evening the pressure in the pericardium, a sac that is around the heart, went to twenty-one. That stopped my heart several times. I did not get any more watermelon until I was out of the hospital and was able to move around.

The constant fight to ward off infection drove my body temperature crazy. I would be lying in bed and in minutes my temperature would go from normal to 106 degrees. I would begin to heat up and the nurse would come in, check my vitals, and see my temperature climbing. The nurse would immediately take my covers down to the sheet, turn on the air conditioner which was in the window above my head and watch the thermometer. If the temperature did not go back down, the nurses would pour water over me to wick away some of the heat. If that didn't work (and many times it didn't) they would bring in bags of ice and put them up against my side, on my groin or under my armpits anyplace the blood was close to the skin so the ice would be able to cool the body as quickly as possible.

When a person is an organ donor their skin is one of the vital organs the hospital will harvest. As I became strong enough to receive skin grafts, the nurses and doctors began putting on the donated skin. This is a very critical part of the burn patient's treatment. The nurses and doctors cover the burned area with the donated skin as quickly as possible. At the time I was burned, donated skin grafts would usually last only about two weeks because it was just like any other foreign organ, our bodies want to reject it. However, it was still the best way to hold back the infection we were fighting against until they could permanently cover the open areas with my own skin.

When the skin grafting process started, I began hallucinating. Although it has been over 45 years since I was in the burn unit, I can remember some of those hallucinations as clearly as if I were experiencing them today. In one such hallucination, I am walking through a jungle. The foliage is very dense and it's all poison ivy (which I'm extremely allergic to). The itching is unrelenting. I awoke to find I had scratched one area of my arm all the way through 4 layers of bandages. Another hallucination happened during an actual thunderstorm that I could hear and see through my window. All of a sudden, an army tank comes through the wall and begins shooting at me and in my dream, I can't move because I am held by vines to the bed. These horrible hallucinations would exhaust me. Following my hospital stay, I continued to experience nightmares about these hallucinations for years.

As part of the skin grafting ritual, my own skin would be harvested on Thursdays. The procedure included shaving the donor area and taking a thin layer of skin. Then they would prepare the skin by "meshing" it. Meshing involves poking holes in the skin so it can be stretched, making it cover a larger area. In 1972, one square inch of skin could cover up to 6-8 inches of area. (Now I understand they can grow the skin for an extended period of time and cover up to 3 times that much area with that one square inch of skin.)

The doctors started the procedure by removing skin from the lower part of my abdomen. The next week they would remove skin from the top of my head. In between the surgeries, they would lay the skin they had removed. This went on for six weeks without incident. Then came the seventh operation to remove skin from my abdomen. This surgery would not go at all like the previous ones.

Mom, dad and I had a regular routine that we went through before each surgery. We read a passage from the Bible and prayed together.

Dad would leave to make the 160-mile trip home to his business and Mom went back to their apartment near the hospital. I simply waited for the nurses to come and take me back to the operating room. This time was different. I was nervous, almost scared.

When the nurses came to take me back for the procedure, I asked them to stop beside a nurse I knew had the same Christian belief system as I had. I said to her, "Please, pray for me! I'm not going to make it through this."

She replied, "Ok, I will, but you'll be fine."

I said, "I know I will. Pray for my parents though." Her face became extremely concerned. I heard later that she actually took the rest of the day off to go pray for me.

Remember Debbie, the girl from Galien, Michigan, I mentioned I was in love with? Well, on this Thursday morning she was getting ready for school and her mother was making breakfast when the Lord laid a burden on their hearts to pray for me. They immediately stopped and went to prayer.

When I came out of the procedure, I woke up to the room bustling with activity. I was in severe pain and listening to some frustrated, vulgar language that I was not used to hearing. I immediately knew something was very wrong. I looked down to my abdomen where they had just taken skin. There was a male nurse on either side of me suturing bleeders on my abdomen. I was bleeding more than normal for this procedure and everyone in the room seemed distressed. When they realized I was awake they stopped sewing for a few minutes and put an eight-pound bag of ice on my stomach to try to stop the bleeding. It would be a long painful time before I got any real rest.

Mom had arrived back at the unit expecting to be able to come in and help me with my meal. She had been waiting for a couple hours when someone went out to her and told her that there was a problem and that she should call Dad to come back and be there with her.

Meanwhile, back in Galien, the burden of prayer was not lifting. Debbie and her mother felt a deep urgency to intercede until the burden was lifted and the Lord had met the need whatever it was and spared my life.

After a couple of hours, the staff allowed Mom to come in. As she entered the burn unit she immediately saw there was blood on the floor coming from my room. When she came through the door of my room, she saw that I was bleeding all across my abdomen where they had removed the skin. The blood was flowing down the sides of my hips, pooling on the bed, then flowing off the bed onto the floor. They were constantly putting new units of whole blood, and units of packed cells (plasma) on my IV poles and running them wide open to keep me safe. From the amount of traffic coming and going in my room the blood that flowed to the floor couldn't help but be tracked down the hall making the hallway slippery as well.

Dad had made the 2 ½ hour trip home, only to find out when he got there that he needed to turn around and make the 2 ½ hour drive back to Ann Arbor. When he did arrive late in the afternoon, he said the blood was still being tracked twenty-five feet down the corridor almost to the entrance of the burn unit.

I remained in this medical emergency from 8 AM Thursday Morning until almost 8 PM Friday evening. Nurses and Doctors came and went, working non-stop. After almost 36 hours and 36 pints of blood/plasma with no natural explanation, the *bleeding just stopped!* Holding his breath, the nurse removed the weight and ice on my abdomen and watched.

In a whisper, I asked, "Has it stopped?"

He responded also in a whisper, "I think so."

In Galien, Debbie and her mom were still praying when suddenly, the burden just lifted from Debbie's mom, and she broke out into praise. She immediately asked God for a scripture that would affirm the fact that I had survived! When she told the story later after all the prayer and fasting they had done in those 36 hours, she was only believing and trusting God for a miracle.

She opened her Bible and let her finger run down the page until she felt "that" was the verse God wanted her to receive. Her finger stopped on Ezekiel 16:6, "And when I passed by thee, and saw thee polluted in thine own blood, I said unto thee when thou wast in thy blood, Live; yea, I said unto thee when thou wast in thy blood, Live." KJV. Later she said she had recognized that there had been another battle for my life and that I had lived through it. Debbie's mom went to heaven in the summer of 2017 at 94 years young. I will always be grateful for her faith and commitment to "stand in the gap" for me. I have faced numerous challenges throughout my life since this miraculous victory but none where God has shown me how meticulously He wants to be involved in our lives.

The next week they took skin off the top of my head for the last time. This was different because they were testing a new type of coating for the gauze that covered the donor area. What they used up until now was referred to as "Scarlet Red." As it sounds, it was a deep red and the donor site took a full week to heal with it. The new stuff they were testing had come in from the Burn Unit in the Army/Navy hospital in Texas and it was a yellow color. They put the "Scarlet Red" on the right side of my scalp and the new stuff on the left side.

On Sunday, one of the weekend nurses came in to check the donor site. She looked at my head and almost panicked. She gasped and said, "Your head has rotted!" A term meaning it was infected.

I said, "No, it's a new thing they're trying." She didn't pay any attention to what I was saying and without consulting my chart she started trying to cut the bandage off. Needless to say, it was VERY painful. Finally, someone else came by who knew what the new stuff was and got her to stop but not before she gave me a permanent part in my hair from the scar of trying to cut the bandage off.

The doctors removed skin one more time, but this time the donor site was my upper leg where the back pocket of my jeans had been and from my right forearm. This surgery would prove to be interesting, also. The stress and apprehension I had felt before the surgery where I had lost so much blood were gone. They had explained that previously no-one caught the fact that my "platelet" count was near zero when I went in for the skin removing procedure. This time, they made sure the "platelet" count was all right and I was confident it would go completely as planned. It did, however with the exception that in the middle of the procedure I woke up!! I remember I was sleeping then suddenly wide awake and something was hurting A LOT on my right arm.

As I started to swing my left arm to do something about the pain, I remember the doctor shouting a command, and I was back under the effects of the anesthesia.

Later in the day when the doctor came in to check on me, I asked him why he had his mask off during the surgery. His face went white and he asked, "So, you remember!?"

I responded, "Yes, I do! I don't remember very much but what I do remember, I remember very clearly!" He apologized and nothing further was mentioned. They spent another two to three weeks laying skin and then the grafting process was completed.

By October, I was making great progress physically. The open areas between the grafts were closing nicely and the fevers had decreased. I was out of the circle bed and into a more normal hospital bed in a semi-private room rather than a private room.

Now a mental battle had begun. The man in the bed next to me spent the night hallucinating. He thought he was back on his farm and had the nurses milking cows and carrying water and moving snow for several hours. Finally, he got quiet and went to sleep. Our beds were only separated by a curtain, so I had been awake through the night as well. When I woke up he was quiet. When I asked if he finally got some sleep, they simply answered, "Yes, he's sleeping well." He had passed away during the night.

The next person to occupy that bed next to me was a boy one or two years younger than I by the name of Clarence. I remember he had a dream of getting out and getting a motorcycle much like the one I had wrecked. Mom and I both got to know both him and his parents pretty well in the several weeks we shared the room. They later came and visited us, and if I remember correctly, he had gotten his motorcycle.

Across the hall was a seven-year-old boy who had been burned along with his brother and sister who were in another hospital. He bit one of the nurses when for some reason he had not gotten his way.

All of this began to cause a mental strain on me. I didn't really know it at the time, but the doctors were watching for it, and that prompted them to move me out of the burn unit.

# My First Trip Out Of The Burn Unit

Sometime just before my birthday in October the doctors, thinking it would help me psychologically with hospital weariness, decided to move me to Mott's Children's Hospital. Mott Hospital and the University Hospital are connected by tunnels, so I was close enough to be tracked but not occupying a bed that might be needed more by someone else.

The first morning someone put me on a gurney and took me back over to the burn unit for my tubing. In the tub room, there was some conversation among the nurses about someone coming from outside the burn unit and coming into the tub room and the threat of contamination. The tubing area needed to be as sterile as possible. At the same time, the opportunity arose for infection in me as I moved from one hospital to the other. I still had a lot of "open" area on my body that needed protection from infection. And, I needed two bathing/dressing changes a day.

There was one advantage to being in Mott Hospital though…food! I learned that every evening a person would come around and make me a cold sandwich and give me Hawaiian Punch juice. At the time I was 6' 1" tall and about 110 pounds. My appetite was increasing, and I was able to begin to enjoy food again.

The doctors had arranged for the Mott Hospital nurses to do my afternoon tubing and dressing change there to avoid my being transported back and forth. The two wonderful nurses that were probably around 5' 2" tall tried to put this 6' 1" boy who had no muscle tone into a standard tub. Not a good scene. The first time they tried to put me in the tub, they dropped me on the side of the tub, breaking open the skin on my tailbone. The morning after being dropped, I went back to the burn unit for the tubing and dressing change. I told the doctors about being dropped and how badly my tailbone hurt. Fortunately, they had a bed available. The doctors had me return to the burn unit.

I just wanted to be comfortable. The nurses were constantly trying to get me up to walk or sitting up to eat, but I fought them every time, especially when it came to walk. Walking was painful. If you can, imagine sitting in a chair, bent at the waist and at the knees with your head bent down; now, put gray tape on all those bends pulling on that skin real tightly so the skin isn't able to stretch and then try to stand up. That is what it felt like when I tried to stand and walk. Along with the pain I was experiencing, I had no place where I wanted to go, so walking in circles up and down the hall was boring and I couldn't get my mind off the pain. Along with the pain was the bleeding. Every time I stood or even sat up, some of the blood vessels in my legs would pop and start bleeding, not a lot of blood and by no means a serious problem, but it scared me to death. One time after giving the nurses a particularly hard time while getting me out of bed, one of the male nurses got me up into a wheelchair and set me in the hallway. He brought me water when I needed it and continued to put the meds I needed in the IV and talked to me from time to time, but I stayed sitting there for over an hour. Over the next several days they didn't try to get me up to sit, stand or walk. This didn't bother me. I was comfortable in my bed. All I wanted them to do was give me my meds (in the IV) and change my dressings and leave me alone.

From August through October there were a couple bright spots. Debbie got the chance to come for her first visit. When the nurses found out she was coming they went all out for me. When I finished my morning tubing, they took a scrub hat and put it on me with my name on it. (In case she didn't recognize me) and put some kind of "smelly" on me. They all made sure they came by and said hi to introduce themselves and generally tried to make it as happy an experience as possible. They did a great job and the visit is a bright spot in my memory even though all I was able to see of her were her eyes and glasses because of all the protective garments she had to wear covering her street clothes. Dad was concerned at first for her to come in thinking she might not be able to handle my appearance but when our eyes met…when our eyes met, we both knew everything would be all right and we were so relieved to finally be able to see each other.

Another friend who was able to come into the burn unit to visit me was my chiropractor. Dr. Combs. He had been treating our family for years and was also a good friend. His visit has brought many funny memories to me through the years. The story starts a couple weeks earlier back in Niles amongst some other friends my own age.

While I was in the hospital, the church I attended back home in Niles was going through a series of revival services. The last Saturday evening was dedicated to the youth and expounded on the evils of rock and roll. I smile even as I write this. The service ended outdoors around a burn barrel where the youth of the church, convinced of the error of their ways burned their Rock & Roll albums, cassettes, and 8 track tapes. Our pastor from that time later told me it was probably a real income producer for the album and tape industries since most people went back out and replaced everything they had burned within a couple weeks. While others were burning their stuff, one of my closest friends had a better idea. Instead of burning the 8 tracks he decided to send them to me! I was overjoyed!

On the day Dr. Combs visited, I had been to the tub, had my dressings changed, been given a pain shot, and was ready for an afternoon nap. I asked the nurse to play a Creedence Clearwater Revival tape. When it started playing, someone from down the unit asked her to turn it up. She did. Then someone else wanted it turned up even more. The majority of the nurses were in their 20's and 30's, so no one minded the loud music including me, so it blasted away. I went to sleep.

All of a sudden, I woke up and sensed a presence in the room. I opened my eyes to see a man in a surgical mask and hat standing next to my bed with some Creedence Clearwater Revival song blasting his eardrums out. When I realized it was Dr. Combs, I immediately asked him to turn down the music explaining that others wanted to hear it, too. He said it was all right but gratefully turned it down anyway. At first, I don't think he really believed me about others wanting to hear it, but when he turned it down and several people complained, I think he understood. We had a really good visit, and it made for a bond between us throughout the years. From time to time he would tease me by asking if I still listened to my music that loud.

Another good memory was my ability to "bribe" the nurses and doctors. Early in my stay, someone had brought in some "Turtles" candy. As time went by the nurses (mostly the male ones) would come by my room before tubing and "negotiate" either a pain shot or warm bath water or who was going to be first in and out of the tub by if (or) how many Turtles they could get out of me? I remember one especially fun time with the turtles.

On this particular day, we had a new to us nurse named Ray helping with the tub room and re-dressing. If I remember correctly, Ray had just returned from the Vietnam war where I think he had been in the medic corps and he was now in school getting a nursing degree. His personality and experiences made him a very "literal" person. I was trying to negotiate something with one of the two nurses named Steve, and I was bribing him with the least amount of turtles I could get by with.

Ray asked, "What's a turtle?" Steve and I had him hooked, and we were about to reel him in. Steve and I started explaining what a turtle was, staying as close to the actual animal as we could, "crunchy outside," "soft almost caramel-like inside;" "all covered in chocolate." We also warned him about the toenails and teeth. By the time they were done putting on the fresh dressings, Ray wasn't sure if he wanted to try a "Turtle" or if we were part of some cult that ate raw turtles. When they got me back to my bed, we talked Ray into trying one and he decided he liked them. From that time on, he had to endure some hilarious ribbing.

By November, I had progressed to only one tubbing a day and the doctors decided they could send me back to Mott's for the rest of my hospital stay. I was there a week or two when Thanksgiving came. Any holiday as a hospital patient can be an extremely depressing experience and even more so for a long-term patient. The length of my stay and what I was about to experience would greatly increase my stress and depression.

Walking was still very painful and hard. I should have been walking laps around the halls and yet I still didn't do any more than I absolutely had to. Everyone was tired. Mom had only been home one time since the accident. She had gone straight from the neighbor's house to the hospital, then the airport to the burn unit.

Also in November when Mom was finally comfortable to go home for a couple days. She came back on Thanksgiving Day. When she returned, she brought a full, traditional Thanksgiving Day meal with her turkey, stuffing, gravy, mashed potatoes, coleslaw, fruit salad everything she would normally prepare for a Thanksgiving Day meal at home hoping that it would create a desire in me to eat, get better and go home. One thing mom ALWAYS did very well was feed us. She brought so much food with her that we had to go to a visitor's lounge to set it all out. We proceeded to "Give Thanks" and fill our plates. Mom dished me up a big delicious looking plate and set it in front of me…and I couldn't eat a thing. All the work and all this wonderful food, and I had absolutely no appetite. When I failed to have an appetite everyone else in the room lost their appetite, too. Because the hospital would not let us share it, Mom ended up throwing everything away. By this time the depression was so severe for all of us, it seemed just breathing was a challenge.

The very next Saturday, came with a lot of excitement. My girlfriend, Debbie, and thirty-five of our other friends, some of them whom had come to church and to Christ since I had been in the hospital, were coming from Niles to see me. One of the benefits of being out of the burn unit and in Mott's was that I could have visitors without the challenge of covering up with the surgical attire. There were so many of them that we had to meet in the cafeteria so they could all be present at the same time to visit instead of a couple at a time in my small hospital room. Up until now, the longest I had sat in a chair was for an hour or so. On this day, with all of my friends around I was able to sit and talk with them for four and a half hours. When they had to leave I was exhausted physically, to say the least, but emotionally it was the best I had felt in six months.

Before my friends left, Dad took me in the wheelchair with Debbie joining us to go back to my room for a moment. Debbie reached to open the door so Dad could push me through it. A man abruptly opened my door, excused himself, and quickly walked down the hallway. My heart was sinking because I thought I probably had a roommate. As we walked into my room, we immediately realized that the guy had been in the process of packing up my television and 8 track tape deck to steal them. Dad took off to catch the guy but couldn't find him.

As dad came back into the room, we heard some screaming down the hall. Dad stepped out to see what had happened. Later he realized the guy had slipped into a stairway and waited for dad to walk by. The perpetrator then took a bedridden girl's television and escaped down the same steps he had hidden in. Dad and I took Debbie back down to our friends. They all left and Dad and Mom, Pam and Andrew and I went back to my room. We sat in shock as the police came and took all the reports. Several months later the police contacted dad and asked him to drop the complaint against the person who had been in my room, explaining they had arrested a group (including him) on charges of drug theft and other more serious felony crimes. Dad dropped everything so the police could continue their investigation and prosecution of the perpetrators.

The next day was November 26, the six-month anniversary of my accident and burns. I don't remember it being a particularly depressing day, I was just tired. Looking back, I think I was just tired of living. I wasn't suicidal, I just didn't care anymore and the incident from the evening before certainly didn't help.

In the morning, someone came to get me to go to the burn unit for my once a day tubbing and dressing change. I'm not sure what had changed in connection with the concern over infection, but there had been no more talk about the fear of germs coming into the burn unit. Dad and Mom had stayed in their apartment with my brother and sister. I was not happy because I wanted Mom and Dad to take me over. I had given them a hard time about it, but I am sure they were physically and emotionally exhausted, also.

When I got to the burn unit a nurse whom I hadn't met before instructed me to remove my dressings, and they would put me in the tub. In the six months I had been there, I had never taken my own dressings off and absolutely never had anyone taken them off dry.

I said, "We don't take the bandages off until I'm IN the tub." She replied, "We always take the dressings off before we get into the tub!"

I responded, "How would you know how we always do it? You've been here a couple days, I'VE BEEN HERE SIX MONTHS!" They put me in the tub so the dressings could soak before I removed them.

A couple minutes after I got in the tub and the dressings were soaking, Dr. Richards, one of the doctors that had been treating me, came in and asked how I was doing. She could tell I was not in a great mood. For the first time, she asked me to remove my own dressings. She then told me that when they got my wounds redressed they would send me home. *Just like that*...like it was an everyday occurrence! This statement shocked me and scared me.

I said, "You mean back to the other hospital?"

She replied, "No, I think it's time you go home and heal the rest of the way there."

I immediately went into the deepest depression I had experienced in my life so far. As soon as she left the room I started crying. I told the nurse, "There's no way she'll let me go home. I just know it." The nurse tried to comfort me, but I wouldn't be comforted. I couldn't believe it. After I got my own dressings off and out of the tub they took me over to the operating room. As the two nurses dressed my open wounds, Dr. Richards and the other nurses came in and out of the room congratulating me on getting to go home. Finally, they convinced me that it was really true, I WAS GOING HOME! I was not the only one who was going to need convincing that they were really releasing me though.

When they finished redressing the four open wounds I still had, (One on each upper arm and one on each lower leg) they had me call Dad and tell him that he needed to come and sign my discharge papers, take me to get my stuff, and that I could go home. When I called, he said, "No, Tim, you just have them bring you back to your room, and we'll meet you there." He didn't believe me. It took quite a bit of convincing to get him to realize that I really was being discharged.

When Dad finally came to the Burn Unit and got the paperwork going, I went back to my room at Mott's where Mom was packing my stuff. While there I had a new-found energy. For the first time in six months, I put real clothes on. For the first time, I ignored the dizziness and walked (unassisted) all over the place. I walked to the drinking fountain; I walked down the hall. The energy I had was amazing. I was overjoyed! After an hour or so Dad got there, and we were on our way home. *JUST LIKE THAT!*

By late afternoon we were leaving the hospital. This was the first time I had been in the outdoors in six months. The afternoon I entered the burn unit I remembered a clear warm day. Now it was cold and snowing. We were chatting away and for the first time in a long time, we were making plans for a future together instead of praying for survival.

# Home To Recover

Home was another hurdle to get over. All the work the doctors and nurses had been doing to change the dressings, bathe me, and manage my medications was now mom's responsibility. I still had four open wounds that would not close, so mom had to cleanse, apply medicinal cream and re-wrap them twice a day. She cooked and cleaned and then took care of me, my 5-year-old brother and my 13-year-old sister. Mom would entertain my friends and family who would come to see me. School teachers and neighbors and the two most active men in putting the fire out at the accident scene came by to see me and share their story.

Dad would come home from working in his excavating business and walk me around the fireplace over and over again to get me moving. I was 6'1" tall and seventeen years old but I only stood about 5' 6". The scar tissue from the grafts had provided almost no elasticity, and I needed to keep moving so the scar tissues wouldn't tighten up. There were grafts on my throat, my abdomen, my knees, and my elbows all holding me back from standing up straight. This greatly hampered my ability to walk. My posture caused me to naturally look down at the ground. Dad would constantly tell me, "Look up!" and "Stand up straight!" as he pushed me to stretch those skin grafts. All this made it very difficult to move around. I would cry and carry on and he would say, "Come on, let's make one more round."

Dad and Mom set up a single bed in our enclosed patio so I could be in the hub of all the activity and yet rest when I needed to and not have to stay in my bedroom all the time. The greatest challenge I still faced was walking. I could only walk in the house. It was cold and slippery outside. I could get to the car in the garage but no farther because of the fear of falling on the ice.

Even though I struggled walking and regaining my strength, I loved being home and the ability to have visitors as well as to be with my family. I spent hours with my cousins playing games and watching tv. My aunts and uncles would stop in and "Check on me" and I loved the ability to be around my sister and brother again.

I think Pam, being the social butterfly she was, loved having all the visitors as much as I did. Andrew not only liked having his big brother around but also having his mother back. People from church would come and sit and talk and let me know how things were going. Debbie would come and spend Sunday afternoons with me.

Being home was wonderful and I was beginning to feel whole and normal again.

Around Christmas time on one of our many trips back to the burn unit for a check-up, Dad got permission to take the family to Florida. It had been a normal Michigan snowy winter so far, and Dad knew I needed to get outside and move around. My daily life had gone from mowing our three-acre yard every week in the summer, plowing snow in the winter, riding my motorcycle when it was warm, and snowmobiling in the cold and snow, to zero activity. Florida was warm, and he thought that taking this trip would get me moving around again and feeling better.

On a side note, the previous spring before my accident, Dad had ordered a new camper. When it came in, he told the salesman what had happened to me and asked him to sell it and he would make a decision about buying another one when this whole ordeal was over. Now, Dad went back to the salesman, told him I had survived, and asked him if he had anything at all available that we could take to Florida to help me recuperate. He told Dad to follow him, that he thought he had just the unit to make it a good trip. Out back, up against the fence hidden from view, was Dad's camper just waiting for him. Dad thanked him amazed that while it was technically still for sale, he had hidden it so it wouldn't sell. Although I was still struggling to walk enough to even get to the car; My parents loaded the station wagon, hooked up the camper and off we went.

Not long after we left home and stopped for gas, Andrew started to complain that he didn't feel well. Dad and Mom planned to bathe and redress the wounds that were still open on my legs and arms. By now Andrew was scratching and nauseated. Mom checked him over and sure enough, Andrew had chicken pox. Mom, the patient saint she was, persevered.

The first week in Florida was cold and rainy. Walking was challenging because of the weather, and the even greater challenge was to get me in and out the door of the camper. I struggled with the steps because of how weak my legs were, and the narrow door would scrape the skin off my arms when I bumped up against it. Mom would heat water up on the little camper stove so she could bath and redress my open areas. Then she would heat up water again to bathe Andrew to help relieve his itching. Because of Mom and Dad's faith in God and their unwavering tenacity, along with the fact that their family was all together, they refused to give up. The second week we were there the weather changed and it got warm. Andrew was pretty well over the "pox" and we could finally head for Disney World.

The first day we went to Disney was on Tuesday. We were there three hours and everything was a struggle for me. My endurance was low, and I was still fighting dizziness while walking, especially while trying to walk fast enough to get on and off the rides there at Disney World. I could walk on my own, but I was still all bent over and moving very slowly. I even forced one ride to slow down so I could get off of it. I also struggled with my appearance. The scar tissue on my left hand was almost black from the lack of proper circulation. My right hand was multicolored from dark to lighter scars and healing skin. My neck was a different color and the fact that I walked like an eighty-year-old man didn't help psychologically. Overall though, with all the struggles I faced, I still had a good day. When we went to the car I was exhausted and weak. Dad helped me as I walked, getting in and out of the car, and then again at the camper.

Wednesday, we stayed at the camper so I could recuperate. Dad called the burn unit and reported the weather and my progress and got permission to move my next appointment back a week so we could go back to Disney World one more day. By that afternoon I was moving around a lot better, and walking was becoming easier! I had almost completely stopped complaining about it. It was a toasty 80 degrees, and I slept a lot.

On Thursday, we went back to Disney World. I walked to the tram and had almost no trouble getting on and off the rides. We stayed for four and a half hours. My energy level and endurance were almost normal for a 17-year-old. I walked to the car under my own strength, and even though I wasn't standing completely straight, I had gained several inches of stature from the activity of the day. I was progressing so much physically and mentally that the next day, Pam, Andrew and I rented three-wheeled side-by-side two-person bicycles and ran them around the campground like normal kids. The trip home was much better than the trip down. Spirits were lifted, my attitude was better, and Dad even let me drive a little bit. Life was beginning to get back to normal. When we got home, I got permission to start school a week late for that semester.

*Christmas 1972*

*Summer 1973*

# Reality Sets In

Going back to school was a very scary experience for me. I knew that my body was very fragile. There were a lot of places where just a touch could cause the skin to come off. One time after a verbal confrontation with a guy, he reached into my car and grabbed the front of my shirt. When I winced, he looked down and the front of my shirt was covered in blood. It scared us both. We both apologized profusely for losing our tempers, and he took me to his house next to the school and helped me clean myself up.

Our school was a one-level, large building. I walked so slowly that I couldn't make it from one class to another in the time allotted. My teachers were very understanding though and excused my tardiness. I continued to gain strength and progressed well considering less than a year before I was fighting for my life.

In March, I started working a job under the Co-Op program. This program provides a student with the opportunity to work half a day in his/her chosen profession and go to school the other half of the day. I worked for National Standard Company as a blueprint maker. I had been in vocational graphic arts (printing) for a couple years prior to my accident. When I was interviewed for the job, the person who was to become my boss had me put my hand on a piece of blueprint paper; then he ran it through the developer. He said, "You have the job. Here you are being interviewed, and you're remaining calm enough that your hands aren't sweating." I later told him that one of the things I could no longer do because of my severe burns was sweat.

In 1973, we hadn't yet heard of Post Traumatic Stress Disorder (PTSD), although I'm sure I was struggling with the aftermath of the very traumatic experience I had just survived. After getting back to school and going to work, I had a terrible temper and it seemed in my mind's eye that everything was against me. Debbie and I broke up and returned our class rings so we could have some much-needed time to adjust to the new me. Everything was a bigger challenge than it had ever been. On one hand, because I had survived my burns, I had a feeling of invincibility, and yet at the same time, I felt like I could do nothing because of how weak and tender my body was. I could walk through a doorway and brush up against the jam, and it would open up a cut on my arm or elbow that would take months to heal. As of the writing of this book almost 48 years later, I still struggle with this on a couple areas of my left arm and elbows, as well as behind my knees.

I hated (and I mean hated) having my picture taken. Every time I would see a picture of myself I would only see the scars and the disfigurement of my teenage body. All of this led to unbelievable stress and a horrible temper.

The more my temper flared, the more things went wrong. One time after getting so mad at Mom for something I can't even remember now, I stormed out of the house and jumped into my car to go back to work. Putting the gas pedal to the floor to spin the tires in anger, I backed out of where I was parked and slammed into the front of my dad's car which was parked behind me. Well, let's just say…some days I was pretty difficult to live with and, of course, there was the stress of having to deal with the consequences of my actions.

In the Spring of 1973, just before graduation, I went to the principal of our high school and explained that I had only missed one day of school that semester and that was for a doctor's appointment in Ann Arbor. I asked if I could get out of my exams and walk through the line with my graduating class if I promised to come back and finish the classes I had missed while I was in the hospital. School policy was if you had perfect attendance the last semester you could opt out of finals. He said I could walk through the line, but because of the one absence, even though it was excused, I would have to take my exams. When graduation came and they called my name and I walked across the stage there was a real hushed applause. I didn't think that anyone would even know my name or that they cared about me at all. I hadn't thought about or even considered the many fundraising events the teachers and students had done for me and my family or the many many, prayers that had been offered up on my behalf. In my mind, no-one thought about my accident or my being burned the 53 weeks before. I didn't have any comprehension of how many people really cared and were watching my life.

I continued to go back and forth to the burn unit for check-ups. Most burn survivors have to go through many operations, especially to release scar tissue that won't allow the mobility that joint needs to function properly. I returned to the hospital for three minor surgeries that the doctors were able to perform at the same time. The first involved simply cutting a place under my arm (like snipping a tendon) so my arm would straighten. The second involved placing a graft inside my elbow so it would open all the way. The last step involved removing the middle knuckle on my pointer finger of my left hand and fusing it with a pin. This was necessary because that hand was burned so severely the muscle was gone that made that finger open. While removing the knuckle made it in-flexible it also made it a more natural grip. They talked about doing surgery on my right elbow, but the normal exercise of my daily life corrected it enough to live with comfortably. For all I had suffered and the severity of my burns, I thank God I only needed these three surgeries!

Another aspect of the healing process was the counseling I received and *yet didn't receive*. On one of my first trips back, I was scheduled to meet with a therapist following my regular medical appointment to help me deal with how much my life had really changed. I went into that appointment with the same "I'm invincible" attitude that I had developed in most of the other areas of my life.

I still had one open wound on each arm between my elbow and my shoulder so when we went back to see the doctor he/she would remove the dressing, check the open area and redress it. As they did this we would talk. On this specific day, the doctor began asking about what brought on all the injuries. While trying to ignore the pain of removing the dressing, I simply said, "I was in an auto accident."

He said with a bit of an attitude, "I hope you had a seat belt on!"

A little irritated with him, I responded (with mock embarrassment), "No, I didn't."

Disgustedly he asked, "Well, if you didn't wear a seat belt, you at least had your doors locked, right?"

Reluctantly I said, "Uh, no I didn't have my doors locked."

He asked, "Why wouldn't you have your doors locked?"

I said, "Well, I didn't have any doors." He looked appalled! He asked, "What do you mean you didn't have any doors?" (Remember, it was winter.)

Again, with mock embarrassment, I said, "I was riding a motorcycle!" He looked at me like I was crazy, and I just smiled back at him.

This crazy conversation set me up to go into the meeting with the therapist with an attitude of "I'm just a little smarter than anyone here." I will be the first to admit I was definitely wrong.

When Dad and I sat down with the therapist the conversation went something like this.

Therapist: "Hi, Tim. How are you doing?"

Me: "I'm doing great!"

Therapist: "How are you feeling?"

Me: "I'm feeling great! I'm getting ready to have my arm operated on."

Therapist: "How does THAT make you feel?"

Me: (a little sarcastic) "I don't know that it makes me feel any way. It's just life."

Therapist: "Does it make you feel a certain way about yourself or your looks?"

Me: "OH?!? I try not to think about my looks."

Therapist: "OH? Do you feel you are ugly? Do you feel like you are a monster?" (I'm not sure about the specific language of this conversation, but I know the words "ugly" and "monster" were used, not in an accusing way but like she had hit on pay dirt and had made some headway with me. As if this was what she was looking for.)

Me (Baiting her): "Yeah, I definitely feel I'm ugly." "I mean, I'm still ugly!" "I've always been ugly!"

Therapist: "So, you think your injuries have made you ugly?"

Me: "NO, I was born ugly and the burns didn't help anything!"

She said, "OK, we're done here." And Dad and I walked out of the office. As I recall, I read her demeanor at the time and for years afterward to portray the fact that I didn't need any help. I know now that she could read me like a book and the fact that I was not ready to receive the help she knew I needed. I regret that someone other than Debbie didn't recognize how badly I was really hurting and get me the help I needed.

When the fall semester was through, I had completed everything I needed to get my high school diploma. By Christmas, by God's grace, and even though we were both young I convinced Debbie I was a suitable candidate for a husband. Knowing in our hearts that we could make it work despite the odds seemingly stacked against us, we talked about making a good life together. We were married in February of 1975. In the years to follow, God was kind enough to give us three wonderful and healthy children, even after the nurse warned Mom I probably would not be able to have children.

From the very beginning of my healing and recovery process, I had the idea that "When I'm healed, and I get better..." everything would go on like it was on that beautiful Friday afternoon in May when I was simply riding my motorcycle into town to go to the bank. I thought I could shake off the accident and burns and resume my life, marry this beautiful young lady, and life would just...go on!!! Life couldn't do that! I was still "Tim" but in some ways, I wasn't anything like the "Tim" of just thirteen months before! Healed does not necessarily mean restored to original. I was healed, but I was also scarred!

When I looked in the mirror, I no longer saw the boy that was halfway through puberty and daydreaming of muscles and whiskers and hairy arms. I saw joints that wouldn't work, many different colored skin grafts, and the body of a man much older than I really was. I was gaunt. I would look in the mirror and think, Debbie is not getting any prize. These thoughts brought on mental and emotional scars that were not in the pre-accident Tim. I built a "super-defense" in my mind with sarcasm and jokes which brought stress and frustration, which then caused anger and temper. I just wanted a normal life... but as Doc Holiday says in the movie "Tombstone," "There's no normal life, there's just life...!"

Debbie was changed, also. She was at church waiting for me to arrive that fateful evening when she heard the news that I had been "in a terrible accident and had been burned so severely they weren't sure I would survive!" What should have been thirteen months of getting to know this "boy I just might like" had become a prayer battle most young, 15-16-year-old girls would never experience. She had spent hours and hours in prayer and wrote me dozens of letters and cards. She learned to love me in a way I have never heard of from any other person or book I have ever read. She learned to love me by being on her knees at the feet of Jesus, pleading for my life! That experience also left her scarred! She was not the same as she had been just one summer before. She later told me when I asked her to marry me, she knew we were too young to get married, especially as soon as I wanted to, but she also knew God had brought us through so much already that He would not forsake us now! That is one of the reasons she consented to marry me less than two years after I was burned.

On February 8, 2019, Debbie and I celebrated our 44th anniversary! (Thank you, Jesus!) We've had 44 years of learning and coping and understanding the mighty impact of the scars we received before our lives had really even started.

That leads us to the reason for this book. Scars! I have a LOT of scars...how about you?

# The Consequences

There is a saying among some people that, "Life happens, just get over it!" I hate this saying! It is telling everyone that nothing in life really matters, and I don't believe that. I think the proper saying should be, "Life happens, how are you going to use it?"

If you have managed to read this far, I'm sure you realize how many scars I actually have, and how many I have lived with for a very long time- not only the physical scars but also the mental and emotional ones. I haven't touched on the times when someone would make a comment referring "to" the "condition" I might have, or the hundreds of times people have asked permission to ask about my physical scars-which in asking to ask, is in itself asking.

If you have lived any length of time at all, I guarantee you have some type of scars. Dictionary.com defines "scars" as *1. A mark left by a healed wound, sore, or burn. 2. A lasting aftereffect of trouble, especially a lasting psychological injury resulting from suffering or trauma. 3. Any blemish remaining as a trace of or resulting from injury or use.*

While this book is about scars in general, I want us to compare the difference between scars and wounds. Dictionary.com defines "wounds" as *1. An injury, usually involving division of tissue or rupture of the integument or mucous membrane, due to external violence or some mechanical agency rather than disease. 2. A similar injury to the tissue of a plant. 3. An injury or hurt to feelings, sensibilities, reputation, etc.*

Let's begin by comparing the difference between the two. A "wound" is something that is still open, maybe festering or even infected. A wound is still in need of treatment or in the case of emotional wounds, counseling. This is easy to ascertain when it is a physical injury. We are constantly cleansing the wound and reapplying salve and dressings to it and when we no longer need to apply the dressings and the salve then we know it is healed.

When it comes to "hurt feelings, sensibilities, (or) reputation, etc." it isn't always so easy to tell when things are healed and when they are not. There's a line from a movie I love that goes something like, "I got a lot of old feelings that I try to put down but sometimes they don't stay put down so much…" How many people are dealing with feelings that don't stay "Put down?" Many of us say the words, "I'm over it." And maybe in a sense, we are, but we keep going back and reopening the wound or telling the story and, in reality, the situation is over but our mind can't let it go. Either the person who wronged us has apologized or maybe we have apologized to someone we have wronged, and forgiveness has been given or received but there is still a *lingering effect*... THAT is a "scar."

Here is the rule of thumb that I use when doing any kind of counseling pertaining to the difference between a "wound" and a "scar." If you are still in the situation, you are probably dealing with a wound. If the situation has passed you are dealing with a scar. Sometimes people will say to me that they have both at the same time, and I understand that. After all that time in the hospital, I had a lot of area on my body that was healed and scar-covered, but I also had some small areas that were still open and in need of treatment, each of which needs to be treated, according to whether it is an open wound or a scar.

This brings up another point. I have people ask me if it really matters what the difference is. To this, I generally pose two scenarios. 1) If I had a

Let's begin by comparing the difference between the two. A "wound" is something that is still open, maybe festering or even infected. A wound is still in need of treatment or in the case of emotional wounds, counseling. This is easy to ascertain when it is a physical injury. We are constantly cleansing the wound and reapplying salve and dressings to it and when we no longer need to apply the dressings and the salve then we know it is healed.

When it comes to "hurt feelings, sensibilities, (or) reputation, etc." it isn't always so easy to tell when things are healed and when they are not. There's a line from a movie I love that goes something like, "I got a lot of old feelings that I try to put down but sometimes they don't stay put down so much…" How many people are dealing with feelings that don't stay "Put down?" Many of us say the words, "I'm over it." And maybe in a sense, we are, but we keep going back and reopening the wound or telling the story and, in reality, the situation is over but our mind can't let it go. Either the person who wronged us has apologized or maybe we have apologized to someone we have wronged, and forgiveness has been given or received but there is still a *lingering effect*... THAT is a "scar."

Here is the rule of thumb that I use when doing any kind of counseling pertaining to the difference between a "wound" and a "scar." If you are still in the situation, you are probably dealing with a wound. If the situation has passed you are dealing with a scar. Sometimes people will say to me that they have both at the same time, and I understand that. After all that time in the hospital, I had a lot of area on my body that was healed and scar-covered, but I also had some small areas that were still open and in need of treatment, each of which needs to be treated, according to whether it is an open wound or a scar.

This brings up another point. I have people ask me if it really matters what the difference is. To this, I generally pose two scenarios. 1) If I had a wound but treated it like a scar, I might simply put a little moisturizer on it and go on. Not using an antibiotic cream or salve on it and not covering it would leave it open for further injury and/or infection. Dirt and other infection-causing debris could get into it, and it would definitely cause the wound to get worse, not better. 2) If I had a scar that I treated like a wound I might continue to put antibiotic cream on it and continue to cover it. While treating a scar as a wound may not be damaging, it isn't really necessary and may hold me back from total recovery.

The difference between a physical wound and a physical scar can easily be ascertained. The differences are not so clear when we have mental, psychological and/or spiritual scarring. What I want to address in the last part of this book is the mental, psychological and/or spiritual scarring that goes along with experiencing an external injury whether it is from external trauma, physical abuse, and/or spiritual abuse. Let me share the Biblical scripture along with thoughts that God has given to me that helped me understand and deal with the after-effects of what I have experienced. What I share may help you with what you are currently experiencing.

# The Origin of Scars

Let's take a look at where some of the scars in our life originate. I think in my mind they come from many places and usually a combination of places. Please realize most of the time the lines between these are very blurred.

Other People.

As we all know, many times the scars or wounds we carry are caused by no fault of our own. We were powerless to stop whatever happened. Not only were we powerless to stop it, but the injuries were inflicted by people we love(d) or who should love and protect us, family members, people in authority, etc. I cannot count the numerous times I have counseled with people who are depressed and despondent because of the damage another person has inflicted on them. These "scar-causing" injuries range from neglect to abandonment to assault. The scars from these injuries many times look almost identical and are not gender specific. I have dealt with children who were abandoned by parents through unexpected death, dementia, and poor choices on the part of the parent. Many people today have been physically abused and beaten down mentally by repeatedly hearing words that cut like a knife. I have dealt with men who as young boys were abused by brothers and dads physically, mentally, and emotionally, robbing them of their childhood and innocence. I have worked with all sorts of people who, one way or another, have been spiritually abused by the church and by the very people who it seemed God put in place to protect and strengthen them. And as sure as I am writing this, I know you, the reader, are identifying with several of these scenarios as you contemplate what I am saying. *Know this*, through it all, God's love has *NEVER changed towards you!!!* His love for you is unconditional and unchangeable. His heart is and has been broken for you even in the midst of your pain and suffering.

Self-inflicted scars.

Some of us are dealing with choices that did not end up as we thought they would, and we carry the scars to prove it, both physically and emotionally. Maybe we threw away a marriage. Maybe we attempted to end our life, and didn't die from the effort, and now we carry some very real physical and/or mental scars from the attempt.

I have concluded that, like the sin in our lives, how we got the scars isn't what's important to God. He wants to respond to you in the same way, no matter the cause of the scar; with *unmeasurable love and unending GRACE!*

As we take a self-analysis of our individual situation, usually we realize that the scars we are dealing with we received by a mixture of our own actions and choices as well as those actions and choices that were totally outside of our control, inflicted on us by others. Using myself as an example, I was driving down the road while looking backward and hit the car in front of me. While that happened do to my actions there were also scar inflicting injuries caused by other peoples offenses. When I am self-assessing my pain and scars, all these things come to light. No matter where the injury originated, this one thing remains true. *GOD HATES IT WHEN HIS PEOPLE HURT!*

God hates the wrongs you have endured even more than you do, even those that are self-inflicted! Since Adam and Eve ate the forbidden fruit, mankind has repeatedly done harm to mankind and *many times* to those whom they should love. We ALL have scars; the question remains is this, "What are we going to let God do with them?"

# The Importance Of The Scars In Our Lives

Some years after I was over the initial physical healing of my burns and Debbie and I were married, the pastor of the church our family attended at the time called and asked me to make it a point to attend church that Wednesday evening. *Little did I know the impact that one service would have on the rest of my life.* Our Pastor explained that he had a friend, an Evangelist, coming to share the story of surviving some burns that he had experienced when he was also sixteen. Intrigued, I promised I would be there.

When I arrived at church that evening, I had only a minute to meet with the pastor and this evangelist. I must say I was sorely disappointed. The man had NO physical scars! When he shared his story, I understood and was very upset, to say the least. His story went something like this.

He was sixteen years old, the same age I was when I had my motorcycle accident, and still lived with his parents who were pastors in the same denomination as the church I was attending at the time in Florida. He was burning some wood in a metal barrel. It had rained, and the wood was damp. As he poured gas on the smoldering fire, the gas can he was using exploded. He sustained deep burns on his face, down his side, on one arm and hand. Like me, he would need months of surgeries and grafting and then recovery time to heal.

Unlike me or my situation, God had a different plan for him. Without going into the lengthy details, let me just say God miraculously healed him within 24 hours without a scar left on his body! *I was appalled!* I was angry that I would have to go through and still be going through all that I was, and God would heal him that spontaneously. He was out of the hospital in 48 hours! The very next day after getting out and only three days after being burned, he and a friend made a trip to a youth conference. The only physical scar he had was on his right arm. It was such a small scar that it was all but invisible to me when he raised his shirt sleeve to show the congregation. The scar was not the direct result of the explosion but that he hung his arm out the car window and the baby skin God had miraculously placed on his healed arm was sunburned and blistered, leaving a small scar. I was almost beside myself with indignation.

After the evening service, the evangelist and Pastor came to me and insisted I come over to the house so we could talk. Reluctantly, I finally agreed.

Before I go any further into this story, I need you to understand my mental state following this service. I felt totally betrayed by God. God had done something for this man that He DID NOT DO FOR ME! The testimony of his healing was so depressing for me that it still emotionally affects me today, even though rationally I know my feelings are totally unfounded. I think you understand exactly where I am coming from here mentally because you may have been there or are experiencing something similar right this minute! If you are *PLEASE do not stop reading!*

When we got to the pastor's house, the evangelist began asking me about my experience. He was amazed when I shared some of what you have read in the first part of this book about the grafting process as well as the physical healing process and the fact of how long it took to recover, and how I was now still dealing with the results/consequences of it all He looked closely at the scars on my arms and asked for permission to touch them. He felt them almost enviously. Then he made the statement that changed my life forever! He said, *"You are so lucky to have all these scars!"*

Forty years later, I still don't have the words to explain how that affected me. I couldn't understand such a statement at first. I believe I was in shock... Then he explained.

He said, "I give my testimony all over our nation. The problem is nobody believes me. Or maybe it's that it is so easy to doubt what I say, but when you tell someone you have been burned, you roll up your sleeves and it is as plain as day or it is as plain as The scars on your body! For me, I need to carry the admission and release papers from the hospital as well as the newspaper articles to prove, first of all, I really was burned, and, secondly, God miraculously and instantaneously healed me." He said, "Your scars give you proof... believability!"

the house so we could talk. Reluctantly, I finally agreed.

Before I go any further into this story, I need you to understand my mental state following this service. I felt totally betrayed by God. God had done something for this man that He DID NOT DO FOR ME! The testimony of his healing was so depressing for me that it still emotionally affects me today, even though rationally I know my feelings are totally unfounded. I think you understand exactly where I am coming from here mentally because you may have been there or are experiencing something similar right this minute! If you are *PLEASE do not stop reading!*

When we got to the pastor's house, the evangelist began asking me about my experience. He was amazed when I shared some of what you have read in the first part of this book about the grafting process as well as the physical healing process and the fact of how long it took to recover, and how I was now still dealing with the results/consequences of it all He looked closely at the scars on my arms and asked for permission to touch them. He felt them almost enviously. Then he made the statement that changed my life forever! He said, *"You are so lucky to have all these scars!"*

Forty years later, I still don't have the words to explain how that affected me. I couldn't understand such a statement at first. I believe I was in shock… Then he explained.

He said, "I give my testimony all over our nation. The problem is nobody believes me. Or maybe it's that it is so easy to doubt what I say, but when you tell someone you have been burned, you roll up your sleeves and it is as plain as day or it is as plain as The scars on your body! For me, I need to carry the admission and release papers from the hospital as well as the newspaper articles to prove, first of all, I really was burned, and, secondly, God miraculously and instantaneously healed me." He said, "Your scars give you proof… believability!"

I never looked at my scars the same way again. It still took me years to totally realize, but I learned to view them as a "gift" instead of a "judgment" from God. This is what I've discovered.

# Scars In The Bible

From that life-changing evening to this present day, I began to watch for Bible stories that included scars. I began to realize that God had given me a gift through the scars I carried on my body that I had not yet fully understood. It took years for me to come to this realization (if I have yet). I wish I could tell you I moved from the Post Traumatic Stress Disorder (PTSD) type symptoms I fought with every day to complete health overnight. I can't say that. I didn't totally. That was a gradual process which I continue to deal with to this day.

What helped me then, as well as now, was to notice a few very beneficial facts from God's Word, The Bible. Let's look at three specific incidents.

Thomas and Jesus. Thomas, who is many times referred to as "Doubting Thomas" was having a hard time believing that Jesus had been raised from the dead. I often snicker when I hear people refer to this story as if they would've believed and can't quite understand why Thomas didn't. But, let's remember, Thomas had already seen several people raised from the dead and healed from severe and deadly diseases, and if we presume he was with the disciples who were sent out and returned rejoicing that "The devils were subject to the name of Jesus," he also had participated in many of those same miracles see Matthew 10 and John 11. Still, because he had not been present, Thomas was demanding proof that it was really Jesus who had been standing before the disciples when He appeared to them in the upper room. What proof did he want? He wanted to see the scars!

Thomas said, *"Unless I see the nail marks in his hands and put my finger where the nails were, and put my hand into his side, I will not believe."* John 20: 26 NIV. Only the scars would serve as evidence of a risen Messiah to him. God allowed Jesus to retain His scars so Thomas and those throughout the Bible who followed after him and needed the physical proof of Jesus' resurrection, could truly believe and experience life to the fullest!

When Jesus was ready, He appeared to Thomas. From what I read, Jesus IMMEDIATELY focused on Thomas and said, *"Put your finger here; see my hands. Reach out your hand and put it into my side. Stop doubting and believe."* John 20: 27 NIV

*Jesus was ready to show the scars to Thomas because it was what Thomas needed and because He (Jesus) loved Thomas so much that He not only went through the ordeal of dying on the cross for him but He also carried the scars so*

*Thomas could see them when he needed to.* When God raised Jesus from the dead, He could have just as easily taken away the scars the cross inflicted. He did for that evangelist I talked about earlier and He was very capable of doing the same thing for Jesus… but *Thomas needed to see the scars* and Jesus was willing to let God use his scars for His glory and to further the Kingdom!

Another time, when people were doubting Paul's dedication to the true gospel of Christ, Paul defended himself with the scars that he carried on his body. While the list of things he had suffered through is in 2 Corinthians, chapter 11, he makes the statement in Galatians 6:17, *"From now on, don't let anyone trouble me with these things. For I bear on my body the scars that show I belong to Jesus."* NLT. People in the Church in Galatia were saying that Paul was not really dedicated to the cause of Christ because if he were, he would be preaching a message of "Grace" AND "Law" (following the commandments and traditions of the Jews) and not just salvation by faith as Paul was preaching. Paul says I have proved my dedication to Jesus Christ and His message by the scars I bear on my body! When you show up where a person desperately needs someone who understands the suffering they are going through and you have gone through a similar situation, God will use the scars you carry to PROVE your experience. This allows God to provide healing for them as well as further your own healing and resolve.

Did you realize that Jesus carried those scars to heaven with Him? In Revelation 5: 6 John describes the Lamb that was worthy to open the scroll like this, *"Then I saw a Lamb, looking as if it had been slain,"* NIV. John could tell from the scars the "Lamb" carried upon Himself, that the "Lamb" had been slain and John knew who that "Lamb" was… because John had been there when Jesus, as a lamb, was slain on the cross. (John 19:26)

1 Corinthians 15:53 says, we'll get new bodies when we die and go to heaven. I personally believe that the new bodies we get won't carry the scars our current bodies do. Here, in The Book of Revelation, Christ, *The Lamb that was slain* retains His scars to prove that he was worthy and provide us with the opportunity to live!

Someone said, "It takes a "test" to make a "testimony." I say, it takes scars to prove the testimony is real. One time when I was commiserating with myself about my "ugly scars" God showed up and said to me very plainly, "These scars you have, Tim, are the signature I left when you were in need, and I met that need." Even though we are to "walk by faith" God in His mercy allows us to bear the marks (scars) we carry so that we are able to relate to others, sharing what God has brought us through. If we will allow Him, God will use our scars to strengthen our faith as well as the faith of others who need to draw strength from our experience.

God says to us in Romans 8:18 (NIV), *"I consider that our present sufferings are not worth comparing with the glory that will be revealed in us."* And then again in verse 28 *"And we know that in all things God works for the good of those who love him, who have been called according to his purpose."* God promises that He will use every situation in our lives for His glory if we will just let Him.

For eight years I served as a volunteer for our local ambulance service. One time I was sent to handle a situation where the victim had spilled a hot fryer full of grease down the front of him. He was burned third degree over at least 20% of his body. He kept telling us we didn't know what he was going through. I asked the police officer who was there to shine his flashlight on my hands. As he did, I showed the guy my scarred hands and said, "I DO know what you're going through, I've been exactly where you are!" Countless other times, I would come upon a situation where I would show others my scars and say, "I can relate to what you are going through. I've been where you are!" By my willingness to share, it never failed to bring comfort in some way to others.

Our scars, once committed to God, allows God through the divine work of The Holy Spirit to use our experiences to do the things God has prepared in advance for us to do, for *His Glory* and provides us with healing in the process.

*"For we are God's handiwork, created in Christ Jesus to do good works, which God prepared in advance for us to do."* Ephesians 2:10 (NIV)

My closing question to you is this *"What scars are you carrying?"* What scars do you need to see as a "Gift" from God and not as a curse of God? Have you been asking "why?" and "what?" and "do I have to carry these scars forever, all by myself?" The answer is "No, you don't!" Jesus,

God's Son, WANTS you to let Him use your scars to provide YOU as well as OTHERS opportunity for a new life. No matter the tragedy, HE BROUGHT YOU THROUGH IT! He is waiting right now for you to allow Him to use your experiences. How do you do that?

First, if you haven't asked Him for salvation, start there. (Note, this step is NOT because of your circumstances or the experiences and/or the consequences that brought on your scars. It is because EVERYONE, regardless of who we are, must come to Jesus for salvation) Romans 3:23 says, *"For all have sinned and come short of the Glory of God."* (NIV) Simply speak to Jesus, God's Son, like you would any other friend and admit that you've never asked Him to forgive you of the sin you were born with (or into) and have committed, and that you want Him to come into your heart and be the Lord of your life from now through eternity.

*"If you declare with your mouth, "Jesus is Lord," and believe in your heart that God raised*

*him from the dead, you will be saved. For it is with your heart that you believe and are justified, and it is with your mouth that you profess your faith and are saved."* Romans 10: 9-10 (NIV)

Second, Ask Jesus to heal you of the pain and the hurt you feel. Ask Him to remove the weight of the scars that you are carrying. God has wanted to do that for you since you first felt the pain of the injury that produced those scars.

Third, Ask Jesus to reveal to you how He wants to use the scars you live with to help others. *Don't rush this. It takes time!* Jesus will use your scars but many times we must learn how to allow Him to. It is a process and it will usually come in steps. First, you learn to live at peace with yourself. Then you learn to have peace with others. Then you learn to minister to others who are hurting like you or have been hurt as you have. As you grow through these steps, remember to take care of your #1 relationship first, that being the relationship you have with

God (through Jesus,) Himself. God loves you and wants to be the #1 relationship in your life. He will show you the way to find wholeness and complete healing.

Finally, don't feel like you must go it alone. I have had prayer partners all my life from my parents, my wife, and my many friends all of whom have sat with me for hours praying and counseling me concerning my walk with the Lord and the scars I carry. This is an ongoing process in my life still today. I encourage you to seek out the help YOU need. Get involved in a group that knows how to deal with your particular scars. In my years of ministry I have personally led and participated in two 24-week sessions of Celebrate Recovery, and I strongly support the methods they use. Through Celebrate Recovery, I saw one man find freedom from scars he had carried for over 26 years from a family member who had repeatedly sexually assaulted him and went on to commit suicide. As a young child, satan had convinced him that somehow it was his own fault. He found freedom from the guilt and heavy weight of the actions perpetrated against him through the help of the Holy Spirit as He worked through Celebrate Recovery and the trusting relationships and prayers of the men in that group. He testified, "I feel like I lost 1,000 pounds. Literally 1000 pounds." He said, "I am so happy, I feel like dancing, and I've never danced in my life." The friend who had brought him into our group grabbed him, and with tears of joy flowing down all our faces, they danced a little jig unashamedly right there in front of us.

What about YOU? *Got scars? We all do!* Will you let God use them for your good as well as the good of others and then ultimately for the Glory of God Himself?

"Lord, I pray right now for the person who is reading this book. Please make them aware of Your presence in their life in such a real and powerful way that they have the privilege of seeing the scars they carry become healing to their situation and pain... and most of all, to bring

Glory to Your name. I pray that they experience Your presence in their life from now until they meet You face to face. For your Glory, I pray in the name of Jesus, Amen!"

If this book has blessed you, I would love to hear from you. You can reach me by email at; myscars4life@outlook.com.

God Bless you, Tim

*Finally, beloved friends, be cheerful! Repair whatever is broken among you, as your hearts are being knit together in perfect unity. Live continually in peace, and God, the source of love and peace, will mingle with you.... Now, may the grace and joyous favor of the Lord Jesus Christ, the unambiguous love of God, and the precious communion that we share in the Holy Spirit be yours continually. Amen!* 2 Corinthians 13: 11 and 14. The Passion Version

# What people are saying about Tim Fletcher and Scarred for Life!

"Rev. Tim Fletcher has been a friend of mine for over thirty years and his story is more than just a true story it is a picture into Tim's life and how he through the power of God's grace turned a potentially perfect reason to give up into a life completely redeemed. Everyone has scars; some more visible than others but a scar is a scar and depicts a major change in the original condition of what was created. Although Tim's are more noticeable to others how they have become trophies in his life because of the power of God is a story everyone can be encouraged by. I had the privilege of having Tim on my staff when he was planting a new church and he has a depth of insight into the Word and working of God and his power that speaks to everyone. I am sure that like me when you begin this book you will not want to put it down. Scarred for Life is a story of overcoming and of victory everyone needs to know because we all have scars. "

 Rev. Bob L. Renner (Retired Missionary Church Pastor)


*"Everyone carries scars with them in life. Some carry more than others. Some scars are physical; others are emotional, and some people carry both. If you are one who is living with a scar or possibly multiple scars from the journey of life, then this book is for you. Whatever your "scar story"*

*may be there is healing found between the covers of this book. There is healing through the author's vivid and transparent telling of his story, and more importantly, there is healing through HIS story...that is, Jesus' story of healing and redemption.*

*I have personally known Tim as a friend and colleague in ministry for 27 years. I have watched him live out his "scar story" of healing and redemption and have witnessed a life of victory despite his many scars. This book truly is a story of victory, but the real story is found in Jesus, the deepest love of Tim's life."*

Duane Roth, pastor

Logsden Neighborhood Church

Logsden, Oregon

having Tim on my staff when he was planting a new church and he has a depth of insight into the Word and working of God and his power that speaks to everyone. I am sure that like me when you begin this book you will not want to put it down. Scarred for Life is a story of overcoming and of victory everyone needs to know because we all have scars. "

Rev. Bob L. Renner (Retired Missionary Church Pastor)

*"Everyone carries scars with them in life. Some carry more than others. Some scars are physical; others are emotional, and some people carry both. If you are one who is living with a scar or possibly multiple scars from the journey of life, then this book is for you. Whatever your "scar story"*

*may be there is healing found between the covers of this book. There is healing through the author's vivid and transparent telling of his story, and more importantly, there is healing through HIS story...that is, Jesus' story of healing and redemption.*

*I have personally known Tim as a friend and colleague in ministry for 27 years. I have watched him live out his "scar story" of healing and redemption and have witnessed a life of victory despite his many scars. This book truly is a story of victory, but the real story is found in Jesus, the deepest love of Tim's life."*

Duane Roth, pastor

Logsden Neighborhood Church

Logsden, Oregon

"Scars — Physical, Emotional, Mental – it doesn't matter. They are all scars that sometimes seem to alter our way of thinking and living. Tim went through a very tragic and traumatic event in his life that left him with never ending painful, physical scars that are visible to the eye. Some of us go through other types of events in our lives that leave us with scars that are invisible to the eye. However, the pain is real.

I have known Tim and Debbie for a little over 30 years. I was honored to be one of Tim's Pastors. I have watched him struggle with pain, both emotional and physical but every time emerging with a faith and spiritual life that was much stronger and vibrant. I honestly believe that this event in Tim's life has given him a sense of what it means to Live a Journey trusting the leading of God all along the way. He is stronger today because of this journey. Tim has always had a non-wavering faith and trust in God but as he describes in this book, I believe he shares the fact that the spiritual life does not take our scars, struggles and pain away or make things easier for us. The lives of Jesus' disciples clearly show that suffering does not diminish because of conversion. But our attention is no longer directed to the "more or less." What matters and what Tim has come to realize is to listen attentively to the Spirit and to go obediently where we are being led, even if we go with scars.

I recommend this book to all. This helps people to see that living with scars can be part of the journey and will strengthen us through the process. Tim vividly shares his story with great pain, but with great joy and confidence that our God goes before us and opens the doors, even when we feel hopeless and helpless."

Rodger Peck -

You can contact Tim Fletcher for your special event or special service. You can contact at [myscars4life@outlook.com](mailto:myscars4life@outlook.com) anytime. You can find other articles and books Tim has written at Pebbles From The Path Facebook page.

## Crash seriously burns boy; cyclist flown to Ann Arbor

NILES — A 16-year-old motorcyclist was seriously burned Friday afternoon when his cycle ran into the rear of an auto on Front St., and burst into flames. The victim, Timothy Fletcher, 1815 Pucker St. Dr., was taken to Pawating Hospital and then transferred to the Ann Arbor Burn Center in a Tyler Refrigeration Co. airplane.

City police credited two men unloading a truck at the Wonderland Discount Store, 402 N. Front St., with smothering the burning clothing of the boy.

Police said they were able to talk to Fletcher at the scene and he told them a car ahead of him stopped and he was unable to halt his vehicle. The cycle struck the rear of the car and fell to the pavement.

Officers said apparently the gas cap was not on the fuel tank tight enough and the gasoline spilled out drenching the boy. Police believe the heat of the cycle engine ignited the gasoline.

Police said witnesses told them the boy started to run and was grabbed by Robert Smith, 35, South Bend, and thrown to the ground. Then Smith, and Roger Briney, 18, of 1228 Front St., who was helping unload a truck, tore off their shirts and used them to smother the flames on the boy's clothing.

Then Smith ran into Wonderland store and got a fire extinguisher which he used to put out the burning cycle.

City fire fighters credited the two men also for their quick actions. Fire fighters assisted police and ambulance attendants in placing Fletcher in the ambulance. The fire department then washed the rest of the gasoline from the street.

Police identified the driver of the car, hit by the cycle as Marcia L. Opstad, 20, Berrien Springs. She was not injured in the mishap, which occurred at 4:40 p.m., police said.

## Two Help Save Boy In Flames

NILES — Quick action on the part of a Niles resident and a South Bend man probably saved the life of Timothy Fletcher, 16, of 1815 Pucker St. Dr., after the youth was involved in a fiery motorcycle accident on Front St., near Ferry St., about 4:40 p.m. Friday.

Fletcher is listed in critical condition today in the Burns Center at University Hospital in Ann Arbor.

Niles City Police said Fletcher was driving his motorcycle south on Front St. near the Wonderland store, when the bike ran into the rear of an auto driven by Marcia Luette Opstad, 20, of 10 Walnut St., Berrien Springs. Miss Opstad, who also was driving south on Front St., told police she had stopped for traffic.

**Two Give Aid**

Immediately following the collision, the motorcycle burst into flames, igniting the Fletcher youth's clothing. Police said he got up and began to run.

Two men, Robert Smith of South Bend and Roger Briney of Niles, who were unloading a truck at Wonderland when they saw the accident, took off their shirts and smothered the fire.

Both Smith and Briney were treated at Pawating Hospital for burns to their hands and arms.

Fletcher was taken to Pawating Hospital, and immediately transferred by airplane to the Burns Center in Ann Arbor. Fletcher was ticketed for failure to stop in an assured clear distance.

## Badly Burned

NILES — Timothy Fletcher, 16, of 1815 Pucker Street drive, Niles, was listed in critical condition in the University Burn center in Ann Arbor this morning after his clothing caught fire in a motorcycle accident here yesterday afternoon.

Niles police reported Fletcher's flaming clothes were extinguished by two onlookers who took off their shirts and smothered the flames with them.

Police said Fletcher was doused with gasoline and set afire after his motor bike crashed into the rear of a car.

When Fletcher, his clothes in flames, started running down the street, Roger Briney, 18, of Niles, and Robert Smith, 35, of South Bend took chase and extinguished the fire. The men, who had been unloading a truck at the scene of the accident, were released after treatment in Niles Pawating hospital for burns on their arms and hands.

The accident occurred about 4:40 p.m. on US-31 at Ferry street. According to police, the motor bike crashed into the rear of a car that had stopped for a traffic light. The driver of the car was Marcia Opstad, 20, of Berrien Springs.

Fletcher's bike was destroyed.

# Students start fund for Tim Fletcher

NILES – A group of Niles High School students, and a number of parents, have organized to raise funds to help a classmate, Timothy Fletcher, 16, of 1815 Pucker Street Dr. who was critically burned Friday in a motorcycle mishap.

Fletcher remains in critical condition at the burn center of University Hospital at Ann Arbor, although he was reported to have shown slight improvement since his admission. He was flown to Ann Arbor from Niles in a Tyler Refrigeration Co. plane.

Students undertook the fund drive, headed by Milo Criffield, to help offset the more than $700 a day cost of Fletcher's treatment. Already the group has raised more than $200 just in donations from high school students.

Three benefit events have been arranged by the students. A benefit dinner will be served from 5 to 8 p.m Wednesday at Franky's restaurant. Tickets are available at Majerek's, from students and at the door.

A benefit open bowling tournament will be staged June 10 and 11 at Timberlanes. Events will begin at 1:30, 3:30 and 5:30 p.m. each day.

A bake sale has been scheduled for June 17 at the J.C. Penney Co. store and donations of food are being sought by the fund raisers.

A Fletcher Fund has been set up at the First National Bank of Southwestern Michigan. Contributions may be sent there or to the First Assembly of God Church 1922 E. Main St.

Fletcher was injured when his motorcycle struck a car which stopped in front of him on Front St. Police said the cap on the cycle's gas tank apparently was loose and gasoline spilled out, drenching Fletcher. Heat of the engine is believed to have ignited the gasoline.

Police credited two men unloading a truck at the Wonderland Discount store – Robert Smith, 35, of South Bend and Roger Briney, 18, of 1228 Front St – with smothering the flames on Fletcher's burning clothing

## Heater culprit

NILES TOWNSHIP — An overheated space heater at the home of Jimmy Juhasz, 1101/2 Ontario Rd, started a fire which damaged the flue pipe, living room paneling and outside siding, according to township firefighters who answered the alarm at 4:05 p.m Wednesday.

## Not so cold

Mostly fair and not so cold tonight, with lows of 50 to 55. Mostly sunny and warmer Friday.

## Police to honor lifesavers

NILES — Two men who helped save the victim of a motorcycle-car collision which set his clothes on fire will be honored tonight by the Niles Policeman's Assn.

Patrolman William Mason, president of the association, said the group will present awards at halftime of tonight's Niles-Holland football game to Roger Briney, 1228 Front St., and Robert Smith, South Bend. Mason said Briney's award will be accepted for him by his mother as he now is in military service.

The two will be honored for their actions when Timothy Fletcher, of 1815 Pucker Street Dr., was seriously burned last May 28 after his motorcycle collided with a car on Front St. and the cycle burst into flames. Police credited Smith and Briney with smothering the youth's burning clothing.

Briney and Smith were unloading a truck at the Wonderland store within sight of the mishap when it occurred. Fletcher was flown in a Tyler Refrigeration Division plane to Ann Arbor where he underwent lengthy treatment in the burn center at University Hospital. A group of his classmates at Niles High School quickly launched a fund drive to help defray his medical expenses.

HEROS HONORED — Niles Police officer Jerry Johnston, left, and William Mason, right, present Certificate of Appreciation plaques to Robert Smith of South Bend and Mrs. Robert Perkins, on behalf of her son, Roger Briney, who are credited with saving the life of a Niles youth who suffered severe burns in a motorcycle accident in Niles last May 28. The awards were presented by the Niles Policeman's Assn.

Photo by Tribune Staff Photographer

## Niles Honors Rescue Pair

NILES — Two men who risked serious injury in saving the life of a Niles motorcyclist last spring were presented plaques by the Niles Policemen's Assn. during halftime ceremonies at the Niles-Holland football game Friday night.

Presented "Certificates of Appreciation" were Robert Smith of 3069 Hastings St., South Bend, and Roger Briney of 1228 N. Front St., Niles. The award for Briney, who is on weekend duty with the U.S. Army, was accepted by his mother Mrs. Robert Perkins of Niles.

The men are credited with saving the life of Timothy Fletcher, 17. A Niles High School senior, who suffered severe burns to 80 per cent of his body when the motorcycle he was riding crashed into the rear of a car last May 28.

Niles police reported the gas tank of the motorcycle exploded, spewing gasoline over Fletcher's body. The youth ran from the scene with his clothing afire and was tackled by Smith and Briney, who ripped off their shirts and smothered the flames.

Briney and Smith, who were working nearby when the accident occurred on Front St., suffered burns to their arms and hands when they smothered the flames on Fletcher's clothing.

Fletcher is recuperating at the Burns Institute at University Hospital, Ann Arbor.

# Tim graduating with class of '73

NILES — 366 days ago Tim Fletcher's future was not only dim, but doctors and family alike were unsure if the Niles High School junior had any future.

His chances for surviving a motorcycle accident which left him burned over 85 per cent of his body were slim. That accident occurred Friday, May 26, 1972.

Classmates and the community in general offered financial and spiritual aid to the young man while he was recovering.

In a handwritten note to The Daily Star, the full scope of Fletcher's remarkable recovery is revealed. "The parents of Tim Fletcher are happy to announce that Tim is going to be among the graduating class of '73," the note reads.

"It was one year ago today (Thursday) that Tim was burned over 85 per cent of his body and was not expected to live several times during his six months stay at the Burn unit at Ann Arbor.

"By the grace of God and the help, love and concern of the many friends and neighbors, he was able to make it. Once again, we say thank you one and all and may God bless you!"

The note, signed by Tim's parents, Bruce and Bonnie Fletcher, 1815 Pucker St. Dr., explained that Tim will have an open house 7-10 p.m. Tuesday, June 5.

Tim Fletcher

Milton Keynes UK
Ingram Content Group UK Ltd.
UKHW021537050824
1157UKWH00050B/604